studysync®

Reading & Writing Companion

Fractured Selves

What causes individuals to feel alienated?

studysync.com

Send all inquiries to:
BookheadEd Learning, LLC
610 Daniel Young Drive
Sonoma, CA 95476

ISBN 978-1-94-973914-5

4 5 6 7 8 9 10 BAB 26 25 24 23 22
C

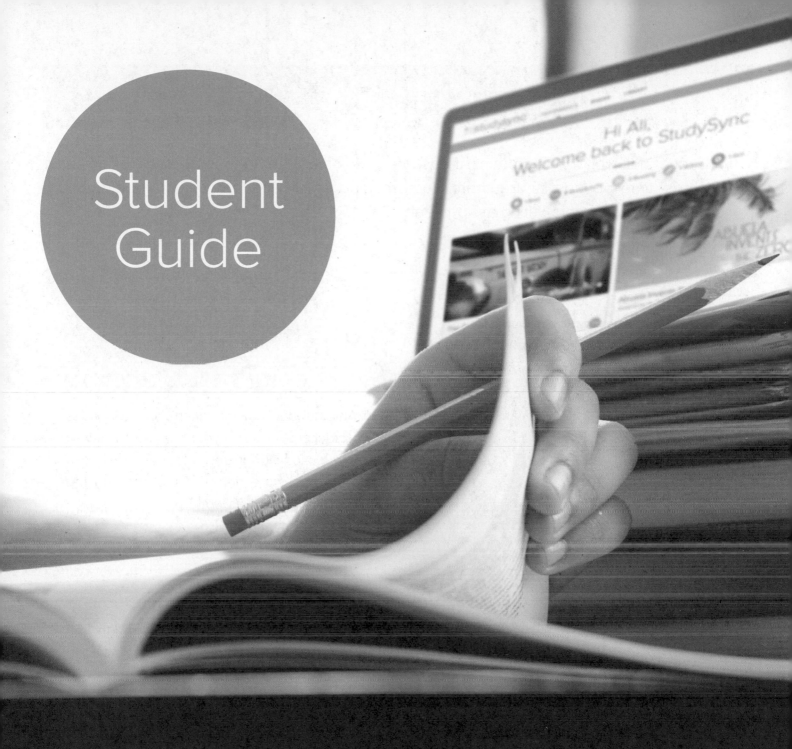

Student Guide

Getting Started

Welcome to the StudySync Reading & Writing Companion! In this book, you will find a collection of readings based on the theme of the unit you are studying. As you work through the readings, you will be asked to answer questions and perform a variety of tasks designed to help you closely analyze and understand each text selection. Read on for an explanation of each section of this book.

Close Reading and Writing Routine

In each unit, you will read texts that share a common theme, despite their different genres, time periods, and authors. Each reading encourages a closer look through questions and a short writing assignment.

Are the New 'Golden Age' TV Shows the New Novels?

INFORMATIONAL TEXT
Adam Kirsch and Mohsin Hamid
2014

Introduction

study tv

Adam Kirsch (b. 1976) is a magazine editor, educator, and poet. He is also a literary critic, winning the Roger Shattuck Prize for Criticism in 2010. Mohsin Hamid (b. 1971) is a novelist, known best for *The Reluctant Fundamentalist*, *Exit West*, and his PEN/Hemingway Award finalist *Moth Smoke*. In this op-ed essay from the *New York Times*, both writers share their thoughts on how contemporary TV has changed how we think about the novel. Through a discussion of the style of Charles Dickens' writing, and an examination of novelistic features, both authors present persuasive arguments for their answer to the question "Are the New 'Golden Age' TV Shows the New Novels?"

Are the New 'Golden Age' TV Shows the New Novels?

> To liken TV shows
> to novels suggests an odd
> ambivalence toward both genres.

By Adam Kirsch

One criticism that could be leveled against quality cable TV is that it is not nearly as formally adventurous as Dickens himself.

Television was so bad for so long, it's no surprise that the arrival of good television has caused the culture to lose its head a bit. Since the debut of "The Sopranos" in 1999, we have been living, so we are regularly informed, in a "golden age" of television. And over the last few years, it's become common to hear variations on the idea that quality cable TV shows are the new novels. Thomas Doherty, writing in *The Chronicle of Higher Education*, called the new genre "Arc TV"—because its stories follow long, complex arcs of development—and insisted that "at its best, the world of Arc TV is as exquisitely calibrated as the social matrix of a Henry James novel."

To liken TV shows to novels suggests an odd **ambivalence** toward both genres. Clearly, the comparison is intended to honor TV, by associating it with the prestige and complexity that traditionally belong to literature. But at the same time, it is covertly a form of aggression against literature, suggesting that novels have ceded their role to a younger, more popular, more dynamic art form. Mixed feelings about literature — the desire to annex its virtues while simultaneously belittling them — are typical of our culture today, which doesn't know quite how to deal with an art form, like the novel, that is both democratic and demanding.

It's not surprising that the novelist most often mentioned in this context is Charles Dickens. Dickens, like Shakespeare, was both a writer of genius and a popular entertainer, proving that seriousness of purpose didn't preclude accessibility. His novels appeared in serial installments, like episodes of TV shows, and teemed with minor characters, the literary equivalent of character actors. "The Wire," in particular, has been likened to a Dickens novel, for its

Skill
Textual Evidence

Before 1999, television was generally lower quality than the innovative television shows after 1999. The pre-1999 shows did not follow complex story arcs throughout a season the way that a novel does from start to finish.

Introduction

An Introduction to each text provides historical context for your reading as well as information about the author. You will also learn about the genre of the text and the year in which it was written.

Notes

Many times, while working through the activities after each text, you will be asked to **annotate** or **make annotations** about what you are reading. This means that you should highlight or underline words in the text and use the "Notes" column to make comments or jot down any questions you have. You may also want to note any unfamiliar vocabulary words here.

You will also see sample student annotations to go along with the Skill lesson for that text.

First Read

During your first reading of each selection, you should just try to get a general idea of the content and message of the reading. Don't worry if there are parts you don't understand or words that are unfamiliar to you. You'll have an opportunity later to dive deeper into the text.

Think Questions

These questions will ask you to start thinking critically about the text, asking specific questions about its purpose, and making connections to your prior knowledge and reading experiences. To answer these questions, you should go back to the text and draw upon specific evidence to support your responses. You will also begin to explore some of the more challenging vocabulary words in the selection.

Skills

Each Skill includes two parts: Checklist and Your Turn. In the Checklist, you will learn the process for analyzing the text. The model student annotations in the text provide examples of how you might make your own notes following the instructions in the Checklist. In the Your Turn, you will use those same instructions to practice the skill.

First Read

Read "Are the New 'Golden Age' TV Shows the New Novels?" After you read, complete the Think Questions below.

THINK QUESTIONS

1. What does Kirsch say about how TV has changed recently? What is the "new genre" he mentions? Use evidence from the text to support your answer.

2. Why do people often compare "good" TV to the writing of Charles Dickens? What does Kirsch say about Dickens's writing that welcomes this comparison? Use evidence from the text to support your answer.

3. What are the reasons Hamid gives for watching more television than in the past? Use evidence from the text to support your answer.

4. What is the meaning of the word **capacious** as it is used in the text? Write your best definition here, along with a brief explanation of how you inferred its meaning through context.

5. Read the following dictionary entry:

   idiom
   id·i·om /ˈidēəm/ *noun*

   1. a group of words, that when used together, have an unclear meaning when read literally
   2. a form of expression natural to a language, person, or group of people
   3. the dialect of a people or part of a country
   4. a characteristic mode of expression in music, literature or art

   Which definition most closely matches the meaning of idiom as it is used in paragraph 4? Write the correct definition of idiom here and explain how you figured out its meaning.

Skill: Informational Text Elements

Use the Checklist to analyze Informational Text Elements in "Are the New 'Golden Age' TV Shows the New Novels?" Refer to the sample student annotations about Informational Text Elements in the text.

CHECKLIST FOR INFORMATIONAL TEXT ELEMENTS

In order to identify characteristics and structural elements of informational texts, note the following:

- ✓ key details in the text that provide information about individuals, events, and ideas
- ✓ interactions between specific individuals, ideas, or events
- ✓ important developments over the course of the text
- ✓ transition words and phrases that signal interactions between individuals, events, and ideas, such as because, as a consequence, or as a result
- ✓ similarities and differences of types of information in a text

To analyze a complex set of ideas or sequence of events and explain how specific

- ✓ individuals, ideas, or events interact and develop over the course of the text, consider the following questions:
- ✓ How does the author present the information as a sequence of events?
- ✓ How does the order in which ideas or events are presented affect the connections between them?
- ✓ How do specific individuals, ideas, or events interact and develop over the course of the text?
- ✓ What other features, if any, help readers to analyze the events, ideas, or individuals in the text?

↻ YOUR TURN

1. What does the author's use of the transition phrase "for instance" tell the reader?

   ○ A. that the sentence includes an example to support the idea in the sentence before it
   ○ B. that the sentence includes an example to support the idea in the sentence after it
   ○ C. that the author's main point in the paragraph is explained in the sentence.
   ○ D. that the second half of the paragraph discusses a new topic

2. Why does the author compare Gilbert Osmond to Tony Soprano in paragraph 5?

   ○ A. to conclude that Soprano is a more likeable character than Osmond
   ○ B. to show a counterexample to his thesis that he then refutes
   ○ C. to give clear and concrete evidence to support his thesis
   ○ D. to refer to a character in a novel that all Americans have read

ARE THE NEW 'GOLDEN AGE' TV SHOWS THE NEW NOVELS?

Close Read

6

Reread "Are the New 'Golden Age' TV Shows the New Novels?" As you reread, complete the Skills Focus questions below. Then use your answers and annotations from the questions to help you complete the Write activity.

◎ SKILLS FOCUS

1. What are the advantages and disadvantages of how TV shows are structured? Use textual evidence to support your answer.

2. Mohsin Hamid believes that TV shows pose a real threat for novelists, and that novelists will need to find a way to adapt in the future. How does Hamid structure his argument?

3. Highlight two examples of supporting evidence in Kirsch's essay. How does the author connect these pieces of evidence to other parts of his argument?

4. Although the authors have different ideas about the role of literature in our lives, they both see a future for both novels and TV shows. What direction would each author give to these artforms? Highlight and annotate examples from the text to support your answer.

✎ WRITE

7

EXPLANATORY ESSAY: Select one of the articles. Analyze how the author uses examples, explanations, and concluding remarks to support his thesis and provide direction to his ideas. Remember to use textual evidence to support your points.

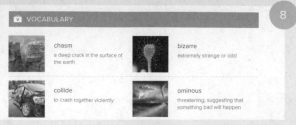

Fate or
Foolishness

FICTION

Introduction

8

An accident creates a violent element that threatens the planet. Can a human and a computerized bird restore things to normal?

◉ VOCABULARY

8

 chasm
a deep crack in the surface of the earth

bizarre
extremely strange or odd

collide
to crash together violently

 ominous
threatening; suggesting that something bad will happen

---

6 **Close Read & Skills Focus**

After you have completed the First Read, you will be asked to go back and read the text more closely and critically. Before you begin your Close Read, you should read through the Skills Focus to get an idea of the concepts you will want to focus on during your second reading. You should work through the Skills Focus by making annotations, highlighting important concepts, and writing notes or questions in the "Notes" column. Depending on instructions from your teacher, you may need to respond online or use a separate piece of paper to start expanding on your thoughts and ideas.

7 **Write**

Your study of each selection will end with a writing assignment. For this assignment, you should use your notes, annotations, personal ideas, and answers to both the Think and Skills Focus questions. Be sure to read the prompt carefully and address each part of it in your writing.

8 **English Language Learner**

The English Language Learner texts focus on improving language proficiency. You will practice learning strategies and skills in individual and group activities to become better readers, writers, and speakers.

Extended Writing Project and Grammar

This is your opportunity to use genre characteristics and craft to compose meaningful, longer written works exploring the theme of each unit. You will draw information from your readings, research, and own life experiences to complete the assignment.

1 Writing Project

After you have read all of the unit text selections, you will move on to a writing project. Each project will guide you through the process of writing your essay. Student models will provide guidance and help you organize your thoughts. One unit ends with an **Extended Oral Project** which will give you an opportunity to develop your oral language and communication skills.

2 Writing Process Steps

There are four steps in the writing process: Plan, Draft, Revise, and Edit and Publish. During each step, you will form and shape your writing project, and each lesson's peer review will give you the chance to receive feedback from your peers and teacher.

3 Writing Skills

Each Skill lesson focuses on a specific strategy or technique that you will use during your writing project. Each lesson presents a process for applying the skill to your own work and gives you the opportunity to practice it to improve your writing.

Fractured Selves

What causes individuals to feel alienated?

> Genre Focus: ARGUMENTATIVE

Texts

 Paired Readings

Extended Writing Project and Grammar

Unit 5: Fractured Selves

What causes individuals to feel alienated?

FAREENA AREFEEN

High schooler Fareena Arefeen was Houston's Youth Poet Laureate in 2016. Her one-year term included delivering public readings in the area and representing her city's youth, and she received a book deal and a scholarship to college. Arefeen, who moved to Texas from Bangladesh with her mother and sister, sees a mission beyond personal recognition in her role. "I want to tell other immigrants, like me, that their stories matter," she says. She plans to attend New York University.

MARCI CALABRETTA CANCIO-BELLO

Miami-based poet Marci Calabretta Cancio-Bello (b. 1989) was born in South Korea and adopted as a baby to a family in upstate New York. The idea for a poem published in her award-winning collection *Hour of the Ox* (2016) came to Cancio-Bello in the process of researching her Korean heritage. She became fascinated to learn about the dying art of pearl diving and wondered if she could be descended from its early practitioners.

WINSTON CHURCHILL

Twice the prime minister of the United Kingdom, Winston Churchill (1874–1965) led a successful Allied strategy with the United States and the Soviet Union to defeat Nazi Germany in World War II. He won the Nobel Prize for Literature in 1953 "for his mastery of historical and biographical description as well as for brilliant oratory in defending exalted human values." He remains one of the most quoted figures in English-speaking history and is credited for coining the word *summit* in 1950.

LUCILLE CLIFTON

American poet Lucille Clifton (1936–2010) is known for her concise language, carefully wrought lines, and the complexity she draws through straightforward images. Her poems confront and celebrate African American experience, capturing the lives of heroes and everyday characters alike. Clifton's work received many awards in her lifetime, and in 1987 she earned the distinction of the first author to ever have two books of poetry nominated for the Pulitzer Prize in the same year.

ALICE DUNBAR-NELSON

The writer Alice Dunbar-Nelson (1875–1935) was born in New Orleans. Her African American, Anglo, Creole, and Native American heritage offered Dunbar-Nelson, according to her writing, a racially ambiguous appearance, which in turn allowed her mobility among various social classes and ethnicities. Dunbar-Nelson published poetry, plays, fiction, essays, and journalism in her lifetime. She is also one of the few African American diarists of the 20th century in the published record.

T. S. ELIOT

Author of "The Waste Land," which is widely considered the most influential work of 20th-century literature, T. S. Eliot (1888–1965) was born in St. Louis, Missouri. After earning his undergraduate degree at Harvard, Eliot moved to England, becoming a British citizen in 1927. He worked as a bank clerk as well as a literary critic and publisher. His poetry was noted as radical and innovative in style, as he gave expression to the dissatisfaction his generation felt in the wake of World War I.

KATHERINE MANSFIELD

Katherine Mansfield (1888–1923) was born in New Zealand and died in France at the age of thirty-four from tuberculosis. In her brief life, she was known as a pioneer of the Modernist short story. Mansfield was very prolific in her final years, and at the time of her death, much of her work had yet to be published. Upon hearing the news of her death, her friend and contemporary Virginia Woolf wrote in her diary, "I was jealous of her writing—the only writing I have ever been jealous of."

GEORGE ORWELL

"What I have most wanted to do," wrote the English author George Orwell (1903–1950), "is make political writing into an art." Born in Myanmar (known as Burma at the time) and raised in England, Orwell knew he wanted to be a writer from a young age. His experiences working as a colonial police officer in India and fighting in the Spanish Civil War inform many of his stories and essays, which critique social inequality and totalitarianism.

LILLIAN SMITH

American author Lillian Smith (1897–1966) critiqued the values upheld by her community of white Southerners in the era of Jim Crow, stating, "segregation is evil." Her 1944 novel *Strange Fruit,* which features an interracial love story, was so controversial that the United States Postal Service refused to mail it. She was an early and ardent supporter of the civil rights movement, and continued to write until her death from cancer in 1966.

TENNESSEE WILLIAMS

American playwright Tennessee Williams (1911-1983) grew up in Columbus, Mississippi and St. Louis, Missouri, and recalls a childhood scarred by his parents' tense marriage. He began to write during this time, and would later base characters like Amanda Wingfield in *The Glass Menagerie* and Big Daddy in *Cat on a Hot Tin Roof* on his mother and father. Williams' plays are known for transforming American theater by bringing forth characters more dark and complex than had ever been seen before.

WILLIAM CARLOS WILLIAMS

The American Modernist poet William Carlos Williams (1883–1963) worked as a family doctor in Rutherford, New Jersey, scribbling lines on his prescription blanks in between patient visits. He crafted the language in his poems to mirror the patterns of everyday speech, which he saw as a distinctly American project. In his epic poem *Paterson,* Williams writes, "Any poem that has any worth expresses the whole life of the poet."

VIRGINIA WOOLF

The work of Virginia Woolf (1882–1941) received renewed attention long after her lifetime in the second wave of feminism in the 1970s. Woolf was a prominent writer of essays and Modernist novels in London during the period between World War I and World War II. Woolf's fiction employed stream-of-consciousness and female-driven narrative. Her book-length essay *A Room of One's Own* (1929) argued for the importance of creating space for women writers in a male-dominated literary tradition.

Modernism

Introduction

This informational text provides readers with historical and cultural information about the early 20th century and the formation of Modernism. The onset of the Great War and the breakdown of colonialism led to unprecedented work among artists who were intent on defying old rules and values. Modernist painters, such as Pablo Picasso, and writers, such as T. S. Eliot, were disillusioned by the manipulation of power and technology and the dreadful effects that the Great War had had on society. Modernists attempted to deal with their frightening reality by creating work that challenged age-old institutions and principles.

"Inspiring heroes and happy endings were no longer a requirement for good writing."

NOTES

1   Throughout the history of storytelling, animals have been used to impart lessons to audiences. There are the trickster gods of various cultures, like the western Native Americans' Coyote, India's Hanuman the monkey, and Anansi the spider from West Africa. Aesop used animal characters so frequently in his fables that it became a defining characteristic of the genre. More recent stories with animal characters are Rudyard Kipling's collection *The Jungle Book,* published in 1894, and George Orwell's *Animal Farm,* published in 1945. Despite the surface similarities, however, these two works send remarkably different messages. In *The Jungle Book,* Mowgli, a human raised by wolves, learns to obey the "law of the jungle" and find his place in their social order. In *Animal Farm,* a group of farm animals overthrows the human farmers and tries to set up their own society. Under the guise of furthering equality, the cunning pigs compete with one another to take over, ultimately creating a horrifying dictatorship. In less than fifty years, popular books went from praising the virtues of societies to making sharp condemnations of their oppressive elements. This sudden change reflects the cultural revolution of Modernism, a movement that broke all the rules by creating new aesthetic forms that departed from the past.

A Shrinking Empire

2   Rudyard Kipling and George Orwell are two of Britain's best known writers. Both were born in India and lived in British colonies for parts of their childhoods and adult lives. Both experienced British **imperialism** firsthand, but they had completely opposite opinions of it. This difference can be attributed to the dominant cultures of their generations. Kipling was born in 1865, and so his views are representative of the late Victorian era. Kipling thought imperialism fueled growth and progress and, like many in the Victorian era, he sincerely believed that the British were civilizing the world. He became known as a strong supporter of British colonialism.

NOTES

Storming of Delhi, Thomas H. Sherratt & Matthew Somerville Morgan (1857). Depiction of the Sepoy uprising (1857–1858) against British rule, known as the Indian Mutiny.

3   Orwell was born in 1903. He didn't witness the explosive growth of the British Empire or see how it brought new resources and wealth to the United Kingdom. Instead, he witnessed its human costs. As a young man, Orwell worked for the Indian Imperial Police in Burma (now Myanmar). He saw growing resentment from the Burmese people living under British rule. He saw the British Empire taking advantage of their labor and resources while enforcing a social hierarchy where the colonists were on top and the indigenous people were on the bottom. Orwell was so ashamed of the role he played in this injustice that he eventually resigned from his job and turned to writing.

4   When the British Empire peaked in the early twentieth century, it controlled about a quarter of the world's population. In the coming decades, however, its control would begin to shrink. The shrinking of the empire began close to home. All but six of the counties of Ireland, Britain's first colony, broke off from the United Kingdom to form the Irish Free State in 1922. India and Pakistan followed in 1947, then Sri Lanka and Burma in 1948, Ghana in 1957, to name a few. Several factors allowed these countries to free themselves from British rule. There was a growth in nationalism and a desire for independence within the colonies. There was also a growing distaste for imperialism among the British. More and more people living under British rule were siding with George Orwell in the belief that "civilizing the world" while pillaging its resources and exploiting indigenous people was wrong. A key part of the Modernist movement was a rebellion against older traditions, including colonialism, and this was partially due to a strong sense of disillusionment, particularly after World War I.

World at War

5   The United Kingdom of Great Britain and Northern Ireland was the strongest empire of the time leading up to World War I, but not the only one. France, having recovered from a series of revolutions and regime changes, began

competing with Britain for control of Africa. Russia, the Ottoman Empire, and Austro-Hungarian Empire competed for control of Eastern Europe. In the middle of all of this, Germany gained power with such rapidity that Great Britain made alliances with Russia and France, despite their being historical enemies. Borders shifted, governments rose and fell, and alliances formed and broke. When a Serbian assassin killed Archduke Franz Ferdinand of Austria-Hungary, it sparked a **conflagration.** Country after country declared war to support their allies or oppose their enemies. World War I had begun.

Battle of Ypres, (1915) by Achille Beltrame.
The effects of poison gases in World War I.

6   The Great War, as it was called at the time, was brutal. Young soldiers had grown up on stories of glorious charges into the enemy line to fight with rifles and bayonets. They were unprepared for machine guns and mustard gas. They did not expect to spend weeks hiding in filthy trenches while listening to the sounds of gunshots and explosions. By the end of the war in 1919, 8.5 million soldiers were dead. More people were killed in WWI than in every previous European conflict combined. The scale of the bloodshed and destruction disillusioned a generation of artists and thinkers who would be central to Modernism. The Central Powers, consisting of the German, Austro-Hungarian, and Ottoman Empires, had all broken up. The Russian Empire also dissolved and was replaced by the Soviet Union. Germany suffered two economic crises while trying to pay reparations, which led to feelings of resentment. This fueled extremism, leading to the rise of Adolf Hitler and the Second World War.

7   World War II was even more brutal than its predecessor, leaving 40–50 million dead. The United Kingdom was among the victors, but it had suffered immensely from the war. Germany used a tactic they called *Blitzkrieg,* literally "lightning war." From September 1940 to May 1941, the German Air Force, or *Luftwaffe,* conducted nighttime bombing raids targeting London and other major British cities. By targeting civilians, they had hoped to demoralize

Britain and force them out of the war. Germany failed to kill the British spirit, but they did do severe damage to their cities and infrastructure. Also, with so many young people dead, the government needed to organize a way to care for the unemployed, the sick, and the elderly. Under the Labour Party, the UK government created a system of national health care. Between this and rebuilding, the United Kingdom had little money left for running an empire. Most of the remaining colonies of the British Empire gained independence in quick succession. Some of the British felt embarrassed by this loss of stature, but others were relieved to be finished with imperialism.

A New World

8   The seeds of Modernism began to sprout before the First World War, but it was between the wars that the movement truly flourished. War had not only devastated the world physically, it was a shock to the psyche as well. The British—as well as Continental Europeans—began to question whether imperialism was really spreading civilization. They also realized that the world was not as beautiful or polite as the Romantics and Victorians had claimed. Improved technology had promised better communication and more productive lives, but it was used to create unimaginable destruction during the war. Suddenly, people felt that everything they thought they knew about the world was wrong. Modernism was a search for a new way to look at the world. Modernists felt that the old forms of art depicting Western civilization needed to be recreated in order to still have meaning. Their movement was a rebellion against old traditions and conventions.

Modernist painter Pablo Picasso posing with paintings and ceramics.

9   Modernism took hold in visual arts before it spread to literature. Artists became less interested in trying to create realistic depictions of the world around them. Cubism, developed by Georges Braque and Pablo Picasso, rejected conventions of perspective, foreshortening, modeling, and chiaroscuro, or contrasting light and shade. Instead, Cubists used sharp, geometric angles to create a fragmented vision of the world. They would show multiple sides of a subject at the same time, creating a new view of reality. **Surrealism** also became popular. Surrealist art, influenced by Sigmund Freud and his system of psychoanalysis, intentionally defied reason by combining dreamlike images and reality. Other Modernist art movements include Futurism, Expressionism, Post-impressionism, Constructivism, de Stijl, and Abstract Expressionism. These various movements did not try to directly replicate a visual scene; they tried to capture movement, thought, emotion, and other abstractions that can't normally be portrayed on a canvas.

10 The artistic and literary communities of Modernism mingled frequently. Gertrude Stein, a writer and leader within the Modernist movement, hosted artists in her Paris salon such as Picasso, Braque, and Henri Matisse, and writers like Ernest Hemingway, F. Scott Fitzgerald, Ezra Pound, and Sherwood Anderson. It was inevitable that Modernist rebellions would spread to the written word. For example, Imagist poetry, which presents an image and lets the reader interpret it freely, has parallels to the Cubist method of presenting a subject from multiple perspectives. Futurism, an artistic movement that captured dynamic movement in a single image, can be compared to stream-of-consciousness writing. **Stream of consciousness,** pioneered by Virginia Woolf and James Joyce, mimics the free-flowing thoughts, feelings, and memories of a person's internal monologue. This style often seems chaotic and ignores strict rules of grammar, since a person's thoughts are not normally as clean and ordered as most prose writing.

11 Modernist writers also broke the rules when it came to themes and subject matter. They would openly discuss sexuality, criticize religion, and violate other taboos. Nothing was off-limits, and this openness was refreshing for many. Many people were reeling from the horrors of war and experiencing a sense of **alienation** from modern life. The public related to stories of flawed protagonists who were overwhelmed by despair. Inspiring heroes and happy endings were no longer a requirement for good writing. This can be seen clearly in T. S. Eliot's poem *The Waste Land,* which reflects the widespread feelings of disillusionment and disgust that followed World War I. Modernist writers broke away from traditional literary forms and values to create the classics of a new literature, wherein reality might be redefined not by fidelity to exterior appearances but by the patterns of myth or the flow of the subconscious mind.

NOTES

12 **Major Concepts**

- **Class, Colonialism, and War**—In the first half of the century, Britain's power was challenged by conflict between the upper and lower classes, resistance to colonialism abroad, and the outbreak of World War I. These years brought a deep sense of disillusionment that permeated British writing, as writers responded to the profound changes in Britain's life and culture leading up to World War II.

- **Women's Rights**—Women comprised another disaffected group who sought greater political power in the early twentieth century. The suffrage movement in Britain, which had long been working peacefully to secure votes for women, took a bold new direction, and British suffragettes used unusual publicity stunts to call attention to their demands. The British government finally relented and gave women over thirty the right to vote in 1918; ten years later, the voting age was lowered to twenty-one.

Style and Form

13 **Modernist Literature**

- Modernist writing was about breaking traditions, both literary and social. For instance, poets used free verse instead of rhyme and meter, and writers challenged social norms regarding social class and women's traditional roles.

- Modernist writers did not view reality as a recognizable constant; rather, reality depended on each person's fragmented or subjective perception of it. "Look within," suggested Virginia Woolf. Woolf and other writers, including Katherine Mansfield and James Joyce, concentrated on writing about "an ordinary mind on an ordinary day."

- Sigmund Freud's system of psychoanalysis contributed to the focus on the internal life of a character and spurred Surrealism and related literary innovations, and his influence is felt in stream-of-consciousness writing focusing on the internal psychological struggles within characters.

14 The twentieth century was a traumatic time for many. Technology, philosophy, international relations: almost every aspect of life was turned on its head. Modernism was a new movement for a new world. The old rules had lost their credibility, so artists and writers needed to find new ways to view and comprehend reality. Modernist writers pioneered a variety of styles and techniques that writers use today. What are some examples of writers, filmmakers, musicians, and artists who continue to break conventions?

Copyright © BookheadEd Learning, LLC

Literary Focus

Read "Literary Focus: Modernism." After you read, complete the Think Questions below.

 THINK QUESTIONS

1. How do the lives and writings of Rudyard Kipling and George Orwell reflect the change in attitudes in the early 20th century? Use evidence from the text to support your answer.

2. How did the World Wars shape the Modernist movement? Use evidence from the text to support your answer.

3. What are some of the ways Modernism broke conventions? Use evidence from the text to support your answer.

4. Use context clues to determine the meaning of the word **imperialism**. Write your best definition here, along with the words and phrases that were most helpful in determining the word's meaning. Then, check a dictionary to confirm your understanding.

5. The word *alienation* likely stems from the Latin *alienatus*, meaning "separated." With this information in mind, write your best definition of the word **alienation** as it is used in this text. Cite any words or phrases that were particularly helpful in coming to your conclusion.

Please note that excerpts and passages in the StudySync® library and this workbook are intended as touchstones to generate interest in an author's work. The excerpts and passages do not substitute for the reading of entire texts, and StudySync® strongly recommends that students seek out and purchase the whole literary or informational work in order to experience it as the author intended. Links to online resellers are available in our digital library. In addition, complete works may be ordered through an authorized reseller by filling out and returning to StudySync® the order form enclosed in this workbook.

Reading & Writing Companion   7

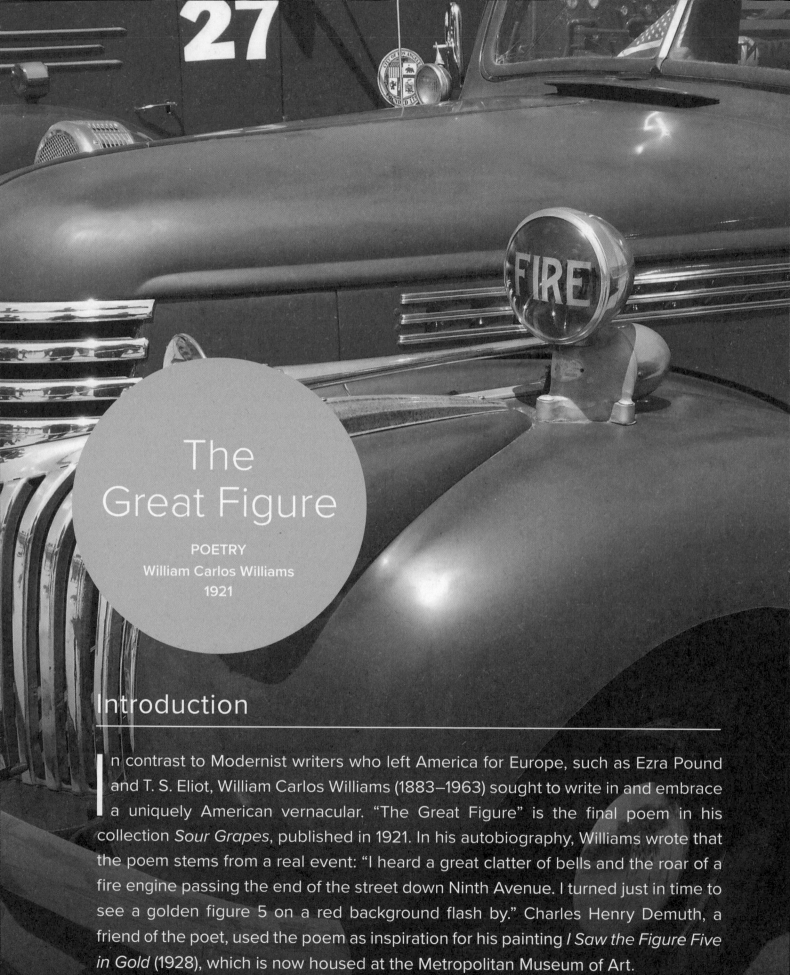

The Great Figure

POETRY
William Carlos Williams
1921

Introduction

In contrast to Modernist writers who left America for Europe, such as Ezra Pound and T. S. Eliot, William Carlos Williams (1883–1963) sought to write in and embrace a uniquely American vernacular. "The Great Figure" is the final poem in his collection *Sour Grapes*, published in 1921. In his autobiography, Williams wrote that the poem stems from a real event: "I heard a great clatter of bells and the roar of a fire engine passing the end of the street down Ninth Avenue. I turned just in time to see a golden figure 5 on a red background flash by." Charles Henry Demuth, a friend of the poet, used the poem as inspiration for his painting *I Saw the Figure Five in Gold* (1928), which is now housed at the Metropolitan Museum of Art.

"Among the rain / and lights / I saw the figure 5"

1 Among the rain
2 and lights
3 I saw the figure 5
4 in gold
5 on a red
6 firetruck
7 moving
8 with weight and **urgency**
9 **tense**
10 **unheeded**
11 to **gong** clangs
12 siren howls
13 and wheels rumbling
14 through the dark city.

I Saw the Figure 5 in Gold, by Charles Demuth (1928) was inspired by William Carlos Williams' poem, "The Great Figure."

Williams, William Carlos. "The Great Figure." *Sour Grapes.* Boston: The Four Seas Company, 1921.

WRITE

PERSONAL NARRATIVE: Write about a seemingly minor event that affected you enough that you continue to remember it. Your response can be a poem, short story, or personal narrative. Be sure to provide specific details about the sights and sounds of the event, as Williams does in "The Great Figure." You may also include your thoughts and emotions about the event and why you continue to remember it.

The Love Song of J. Alfred Prufrock

POETRY
T.S. Eliot
1915

Introduction

Born in St. Louis to an old New England family, T. S. Eliot (1888–1965) was educated at Harvard, the Sorbonne, and Oxford, and received the Nobel Prize for Literature in 1948 for his boldly innovative and influential style. "The Love Song of J. Alfred Prufrock" demonstrates Eliot's characteristic stream of consciousness and versatility with diction. The poem marked a shift in poetic tradition from Romantic verse and Georgian lyrics to Modernism. Filled with allusions to other written works, Elliot takes the reader on a sentimental journey of a gentleman as he questions his life and worth.

"I should have been a pair of ragged claws Scuttling across the floors of silent seas."

Skill:
Poetic Elements
and Structure

*Eliot begins the poem
with an epigraph that is
in another language.
This epigraph is most
likely from another
literary work. Eliot
assumes that his
reader can read this
other language or is
familiar with the work.*

"The Love Song of J. Alfred Prufrock"

1   *S'io credesse che mia risposta fosse*
2   *A persona che mai tornasse al mondo,*
3   *Questa fiamma staria senza piu scosse.*
4   *Ma perciocche giammai di questo fondo*
5   *Non torno vivo alcun, s'i'odo il vero,*
6   *Senza tema d'infamia ti rispondo.*

7   Let us go then, you and I,
8   When the evening is spread out against the sky
9   Like a patient **etherized** upon a table;
10 Let us go, through certain half-deserted streets,
11 The muttering retreats
12 Of restless nights in one-night cheap hotels
13 And sawdust restaurants with oyster-shells:
14 Streets that follow like a **tedious** argument
15 Of **insidious** intent
16 To lead you to an overwhelming question . . .
17 Oh, do not ask, "What is it?"
18 Let us go and make our visit.

19 In the room the women come and go
20 Talking of Michelangelo[1].

21 The yellow fog that rubs its back upon the window-panes,
22 The yellow smoke that rubs its muzzle on the window-panes
23 Licked its tongue into the corners of the evening,
24 Lingered upon the pools that stand in drains,
25 Let fall upon its back the soot that falls from chimneys,
26 Slipped by the terrace, made a sudden leap,

T.S. Eliot

---

1. **Michelangelo** Michelangelo di Lodovico Buonarroti Simoni (1475–1564), Renaissance artist and sculptor, whose most famous works include David and the ceiling of the Sistine Chapel in Rome

27 And seeing that it was a soft October night,
28 Curled once about the house, and fell asleep.

29 And indeed there will be time
30 For the yellow smoke that slides along the street,
31 Rubbing its back upon the window panes;
32 There will be time, there will be time
33 To prepare a face to meet the faces that you meet
34 There will be time to murder and create,
35 And time for all the works and days of hands
36 That lift and drop a question on your plate;
37 Time for you and time for me,
38 And time yet for a hundred indecisions,
39 And for a hundred visions and revisions,
40 Before the taking of a toast and tea.

41 In the room the women come and go
42 Talking of Michelangelo.

43 And indeed there will be time
44 To wonder, "Do I dare?" and, "Do I dare?"
45 Time to turn back and descend the stair,
46 With a bald spot in the middle of my hair—
47 (They will say: "How his hair is growing thin!")
48 My morning coat, my collar mounting firmly to the chin,
49 My necktie rich and modest, but asserted by a simple pin—
50 (They will say: "But how his arms and legs are thin!")
51 Do I dare
52 Disturb the universe?
53 In a minute there is time
54 For decisions and revisions which a minute will reverse.

55 For I have known them all already, known them all:
56 Have known the evenings, mornings, afternoons,
57 I have measured out my life with coffee spoons;
58 I know the voices dying with a dying fall
59 Beneath the music from a farther room.
60 So how should I presume?

61 And I have known the eyes already, known them all—
62 The eyes that fix you in a formulated phrase,
63 And when I am formulated, sprawling on a pin,
64 When I am pinned and wriggling on the wall,
65 Then how should I begin
66 To spit out all the butt-ends of my days and ways?
67 And how should I presume?

Skill:
Poetic Elements
and Structure

Eliot uses repetition and rhyming couplets to give details about Prufrock's appearance. He is dressed well, but he worries about what people say about him, imagining they focus on his "bald spot" and thin arms and legs.

68   And I have known the arms already, known them all—
69   Arms that are braceleted and white and bare
70   (But in the lamplight, downed with light brown hair!)
71   Is it perfume from a dress
72   That makes me so digress?
73   Arms that lie along a table, or wrap about a shawl.
74   And should I then presume?
75   And how should I begin?

. . .

Skill:
Poetic Elements
and Structure

The metaphor shows
that Prufrock feels he
should have been a
creature at the bottom
of the sea. The "lonely
men" that Prufrock
sees support the sense
of isolation. Each line
ends in "s" and the "s"
sound is repeated
throughout.

76   Shall I say, I have gone at dusk through narrow streets
77   And watched the smoke that rises from the pipes
78   Of lonely men in shirt-sleeves, leaning out of windows?

79   I should have been a pair of ragged claws
80   Scuttling across the floors of silent seas.

. . .

81   And the afternoon, the evening, sleeps so peacefully!
82   Smoothed by long fingers,
83   Asleep . . . tired . . . or it **malingers**.
84   Stretched on the floor, here beside you and me.
85   Should I, after tea and cakes and ices,
86   Have the strength to force the moment to its crisis?
87   But though I have wept and fasted, wept and prayed,
88   Though I have seen my head (grown slightly bald) brought in upon a platter,
89   I am no prophet—and here's no great matter;
90   I have seen the moment of my greatness flicker,
91   And I have seen the eternal Footman[2] hold my coat, and snicker,
92   And in short, I was afraid.

93   And would it have been worth it, after all,
94   After the cups, the marmalade, the tea,
95   Among the porcelain, among some talk of you and me,
96   Would it have been worth while,
97   To have bitten off the matter with a smile,
98   To have squeezed the universe into a ball
99   To roll it toward some overwhelming question,
100 To say: "I am Lazarus[3], come from the dead,
101 Come back to tell you all, I shall tell you all"—

2. **footman** a house servant who attends to guests, as a porter might in a hotel
3. **Lazarus** Biblical figure raised from the dead by Jesus Christ

102 If one, settling a pillow by her head,
103 Should say: "That is not what I meant at all;
105 That is not it, at all."

105 And would it have been worth it, after all,
106 Would it have been worth while,
107 After the sunsets and the dooryards and the sprinkled streets,
108 After the novels, after the teacups, after the skirts that trail along the floor—
109 And this, and so much more?—
110 It is impossible to say just what I mean!
111 But as if a magic lantern threw the nerves in patterns on a screen:
112 Would it have been worth while
113 If one, settling a pillow or throwing off a shawl,
114 And turning toward the window, should say:
115 "That is not it at all,
116 That is not what I meant, at all."

. . .

177 No! I am not Prince Hamlet, nor was meant to be;
118 Am an attendant lord, one that will do
119 To swell a progress, start a scene or two,
120 Advise the prince; no doubt, an easy tool,
121 Deferential, glad to be of use,
122 Politic, cautious, and meticulous;
123 Full of high sentence, but a bit obtuse;
124 At times, indeed, almost ridiculous—
125 Almost, at times, the Fool[4].

126 I grow old . . . I grow old . . .
127 I shall wear the bottoms of my trousers rolled.

128 Shall I part my hair behind? Do I dare to eat a peach?
129 I shall wear white flannel trousers, and walk upon the beach.
130 I have heard the mermaids singing, each to each.

131 I do not think that they will sing to me.

132 I have seen them riding seaward on the waves
133 Combing the white hair of the waves blown back
134 When the wind blows the water white and black.

135 We have lingered in the chambers of the sea
136 By sea-girls wreathed with seaweed red and brown
137 Till human voices wake us, and we drown.

 Skill:
Language, Style,
and Audience

The speaker's allusion to Shakespeare's Hamlet effectively shows that he views himself as absurd and awkward. He was not "meant to be" a prince like Hamlet, but instead thinks of himself as "the Fool."

---

4. **the Fool** a character in a Tarot deck—a counterpart to the Joker in a deck of playing cards—
   depicted by an illustration of a young man at the edge of a cliff

First Read

Read "The Love Song of J. Alfred Prufrock." After you read, complete the Think Questions below.

 THINK QUESTIONS

1. What phrases or lines are repeated in the poem? What do these repetitions tell you about the speaker of the poem? Support your response with evidence from the text.

2. How is the speaker's appearance described? What can you infer about Prufrock from these descriptions? Support your response with evidence from the text.

3. Write two or three sentences summarizing the events of the poem. What seems to occur in the time span of the poem? Use evidence from the text to support your response.

4. Use context clues to determine the meaning of the word **malingers** as it is used in "The Love Song of J. Alfred Prufrock." Write your definition of *malingers* here and explain how you arrived at this definition.

5. Use context clues to determine the meaning of the word **deferential** as it is used in "The Love Song of J. Alfred Prufrock." Write your definition of *deferential* here and explain how you arrived at this definition.

Skill:
Language, Style, and Audience

Use the Checklist to analyze Language, Style, and Audience in "The Love Song of J. Alfred Prufrock." Refer to the sample student annotations about Language, Style, and Audience in the text.

••• CHECKLIST FOR LANGUAGE, STYLE, AND AUDIENCE

In order to determine an author's style and possible intended audience, do the following:

- ✓ identify language that is particularly fresh, engaging, or beautiful

- ✓ analyze the surrounding words and phrases as well as the context in which the specific words are being used

- ✓ note the audience—both intended and unintended—and possible reactions to the author's word choice and style

- ✓ note any allusions the author makes to texts written by other authors

- ✓ examine your reaction to the author's word choice and how the author's choice affected your reaction

To analyze the impact of a specific word choice on meaning including words with multiple meanings or language that is particularly fresh, engaging, or beautiful, consider the following questions:

- ✓ How does the author's use of fresh, engaging, or beautiful language enhance or change what is being described? How would a specific phrase or sentence sound different or shift in meaning if a synonym were used?

- ✓ How does the rhyme scheme, meter, and other poetic language affect the meaning?

- ✓ How does word choice, including different possible meanings from other countries, help determine meaning?

- ✓ How does the author use poetic techniques, multiple meaning words, and language that appeals to emotions to craft a message or idea?

- ✓ How would the text be different if another type of technique or other words were used?

Skill:
Language, Style, and Audience

Reread Lines 105–116 of "The Love Song of J. Alfred Prufrock." Then, using the Checklist on the previous page, answer the multiple-choice questions below.

↻ YOUR TURN

1. What is the most likely interpretation of "But as if a magic lantern threw the nerves in patterns on a screen"?

   ○ A. Prufrock can explain himself so clearly that it is like being able to read words on a screen.

   ○ B. Prufrock's emotions are so clear to him that it is like seeing his nervous system on a screen.

   ○ C. Prufrock's nervousness is so intense that it seems his nerves are being projected onto a screen.

   ○ D. Prufrock sees himself as a magician who can make patterns seem to appear and change on a screen.

2. Which statement best evaluates how the author's use of language affects the reader's perception of Prufrock in these lines?

   ○ A. The author's choice to use repetition emphasizes Prufrock's uncertainty about how to communicate what he is trying to say.

   ○ B. The author's choice to include a sentence that asks a question is effective because the purpose of the poem is to make a request of readers.

   ○ C. The language in line 113 helps readers understand that Prufrock is lying in bed as he writes the poem.

   ○ D. The author's lists in lines 107 and 108 are distracting because readers do not know enough about the events he is referencing.

Skill:
Poetic Elements and Structure

Use the Checklist to analyze Poetic Elements and Structure in "The Love Song of J. Alfred Prufrock." Refer to the sample student annotations about Poetic Elements and Structure in the text.

> ••• CHECKLIST FOR POETIC ELEMENTS AND STRUCTURE

In order to analyze a poet's choices concerning how to structure specific parts of a poem, note the following:

- ✓ the form and overall structure of the poem

- ✓ the rhyme, rhythm, and meter, if present

- ✓ lines and stanzas in the poem that suggest its meanings and aesthetic impact

- ✓ how the poet began or ended the poem

- ✓ if the poet provided a comedic or tragic resolution

To analyze how an author's choices concerning how to structure specific parts of a poem contribute to its overall structure and meaning as well as its aesthetic impact, consider the following questions:

- ✓ How does the poet structure the poem? What is the structure of specific parts?

- ✓ How do the poet's choices contribute to the poem's overall structure, meaning, and aesthetic impact?

Please note that excerpts and passages in the StudySync® library and this workbook are intended as touchstones to generate interest in an author's work. The excerpts and passages do not substitute for the reading of entire texts, and StudySync® strongly recommends that students seek out and purchase the whole literary or informational work in order to experience it as the author intended. Links to online resellers are available in our digital library. In addition, complete works may be ordered through an authorized reseller by filling out and returning to StudySync® the order form enclosed in this workbook.

Reading & Writing Companion

19

Skill:
Poetic Elements and Structure

Reread lines 127–138 of "The Love Song of J. Alfred Prufrock." Then, using the Checklist on the previous page, answer the multiple-choice questions below.

⟳ YOUR TURN

1. This question has two parts. First, answer Part A. Then, answer Part B.

   Part A: Which statement best describes the rhyme scheme of these lines?

   ○ A. Eliot mainly uses couplets with some lines that break the pattern.

   ○ B. Eliot does not use a consistent rhyme scheme, even though some words rhyme.

   ○ C. Eliot follows a traditional rhyme scheme of *aabba*, which is usually found in sonnets.

   ○ D. Eliot uses blank verse to allude to the work of famous English poets who came before him.

   Part B: Which statement explains why Eliot would choose to use the rhyme scheme in Part A?

   ○ A. Eliot wanted to write a poem that completely rejected traditional poetic structures.

   ○ B. Eliot wanted to align himself with famous English writers like Shakespeare and Milton.

   ○ C. Eliot wanted to draw the reader's attention to the lines that do not fit the rhyme scheme.

   ○ D. Eliot wanted to help the reader follow the poem's conclusion by using a set rhyme scheme.

2. Which statement best explains a possible reason Eliot ended the poem as he did?

   ○ A. After focusing on Prufrock's regrets and insecurities, Eliot ended the poem on a hopeful note.

   ○ B. Prufrock is mostly unable to take action, but Eliot ends the poem with Prufrock in love.

   ○ C. The poem's conclusion offers Eliot's answer to Prufrock's question about how to begin.

   ○ D. Eliot wanted to highlight that Prufrock is unable to change by the poem's conclusion.

Skill:
Compare and Contrast

Use the Checklist to analyze Compare and Contrast in "The Love Song of J. Alfred Prufrock."

••• CHECKLIST FOR COMPARE AND CONTRAST

In order to determine how to compare and contrast texts from the same period, and how these texts treat similar themes or topics, use the following steps:

✓ first, identify two or more foundational works of American literature written during the eighteenth-, nineteenth- or early-twentieth-century

✓ next, identify the topic and theme in each work, and any central or recurring topics the author presents

✓ after, explain how each text reflects and represents the time period in which it was written, including its historical events, customs, beliefs, or social norms

✓ finally, explain the similarities or differences between two or more texts that are written during the same time period and address related themes and topics

To demonstrate knowledge of eighteenth-, nineteenth- and early-twentieth-century foundational works of American literature, consider the following questions:

✓ Are the texts from the same time period in American literature?

✓ In what ways does each text reflect and represent the time period in which it was written?

✓ How does each work treat themes or topics representative of the time period in which it was written?

✓ How is the treatment of the themes or topics in these literary works similar and different?

Please note that excerpts and passages in the StudySync® library and this workbook are intended as touchstones to generate interest in an author's work. The excerpts and passages do not substitute for the reading of entire texts, and StudySync® strongly recommends that students seek out and purchase the whole literary or informational work in order to experience it as the author intended. Links to online resellers are available in our digital library. In addition, complete works may be ordered through an authorized reseller by filling out and returning to StudySync® the order form enclosed in this workbook.

Reading & Writing
Companion

21

Skill:
Compare and Contrast

Reread lines 7–18 of "The Love Song of J. Alfred Prufrock" and the entirety of "The Great Figure." Then, answer the multiple-choice questions that follow.

🔄 YOUR TURN

1. What theme, common to Modernism, do you see in these lines from both poems?

   ○ A. The chaos of modern life can sometimes make one feel isolated and overwhelmed.
   ○ B. One should be fearful of the technology and industrialization at the center of modern life.
   ○ C. Those who are tasked with protecting others grow accustomed to chaotic experiences.
   ○ D. The world seems forever dark and cold to those who are too afraid to love.

2. Which statement best compares the use of sentence structure in both poems?

   ○ A. Both poems reject traditional punctuation to allow readers to follow the flow of ideas.
   ○ B. Both poems experiment with sentence structure to show the positive outlook of the speaker.
   ○ C. Both poems use a combination of very short and very long sentences to highlight main ideas.
   ○ D. Both poems use long and fragmented sentence structure to show new thoughts entering the text.

Close Read

Reread "The Love Song of J. Alfred Prufrock." As you reread, complete the Skills Focus questions below. Then use your answers and annotations from the questions to help you complete the Write activity.

◎ SKILLS FOCUS

1. Highlight a section in the beginning of the poem in which the speaker uses multiple meanings or engaging language to describe the evening. Describe the effect the poet's word choice has on the reader's understanding of the scene.

2. Identify a section in which the poet includes a description that evokes at least one of the five senses. Explain why this description is effective and how it shapes your perception of the text.

3. Identify a section in which the poet uses unconventional sentence or poetic structure. Explain why this unconventional structure is effective and how it shapes your perception of the text.

4. Highlight a section in which the speaker is shown to be overwhelmed. Using your memory, compare this to the speaker's emotions in "The Great Figure." Explain how the behavior of each speaker reflects the poem's literary period

5. The title "The Love Song of J. Alfred Prufrock" might seem misleading after reading the poem. Identify two moments in which the speaker of the poem expresses a feeling of alienation. What causes his alienation? Why is this poem called a "Love Song"?

✏ WRITE

LITERARY ANALYSIS: Some critics claim that the speaker in "The Love Song of J. Alfred Prufrock" describes an atmosphere that is his own personal hell. What evidence in the poem do you find to support this claim? What is it about Prufrock's existence that seems hellish, and how does that existence help define this poem as a Modernist poem? Write a response that answers these questions, using evidence from the text to support your ideas.

Please note that excerpts and passages in the StudySync® library and this workbook are intended as touchstones to generate interest in an author's work. The excerpts and passages do not substitute for the reading of entire texts, and StudySync® strongly recommends that students seek out and purchase the whole literary or informational work in order to experience it as the author intended. Links to online resellers are available in our digital library. In addition, complete works may be ordered through an authorized reseller by filling out and returning to StudySync® the order form enclosed in this workbook.

Reading & Writing Companion   **23**

miss rosie

POETRY
Lucille Clifton
1987

Introduction

Twice a finalist for the Pulitzer Prize in Poetry, American poet and educator Lucille Clifton (1936–2010) was born in Depew, New York. In addition to offering acute insight into family dynamics, community, and the African American experience, Clifton's work is often heralded for its exploration of the enduring strength and dignity of those who live on the margins of society. One such poem, "miss rosie," tells the story of someone who, on the surface, appears to be a homeless woman whom people might pass by, leaving her forlorn and forgotten. Yet, as we learn from the speaker, people are more than their present circumstances.

"through your destruction / i stand up"

NOTES

1 when i watch you
2 wrapped up like garbage
3 sitting, surrounded by the smell
4 of too old potato peels
5 or
6 when i watch you
7 in your old man's shoes
8 with the little toe cut out
9 sitting, waiting for your mind
10 like next week's grocery
11 i say
12 when i watch you
13 you wet brown bag of a woman
14 who used to be the best looking gal in georgia
15 used to be called the Georgia Rose
16 i stand up
17 through your destruction
18 i stand up

Lucille Clifton, "miss rosie" from The Collected Poems of Lucille Clifton. Copyright © 1987 by Lucille Clifton. Reprinted with the permission of The Permissions Company, Inc., on behalf of BOA Editions, Ltd., www.boaeditions.org.

✏ WRITE

LITERARY ANALYSIS: The poem "miss rosie" follows a dramatic structure as the speaker recounts the life of a person that society often ignores. Write a short response in which you analyze the effect the dramatic structure has on the meaning of the poem. In your essay, consider and respond to questions such as the following: What story does this poem tell? What relationship does the speaker of the poem have with Miss Rosie? How would the story be different if Miss Rosie were telling her own story? What message is being conveyed by this story? Remember to use textual evidence to support your response.

Please note that excerpts and passages in the StudySync® library and this workbook are intended as touchstones to generate interest in an author's work. The excerpts and passages do not substitute for the reading of entire texts, and StudySync® strongly recommends that students seek out and purchase the whole literary or informational work in order to experience it as the author intended. Links to online resellers are available in our digital library. In addition, complete works may be ordered through an authorized reseller by filling out and returning to StudySync® the order form enclosed in this workbook.

Reading & Writing Companion

25

The Idler

POETRY
Alice Dunbar-Nelson
1895

Introduction

Poet, essayist, diarist, and activist Alice Dunbar-Nelson (1875–1935) was born in New Orleans, Louisiana, the daughter of a once-enslaved Louisiana woman named Patricia Wright. Identity, family and oppression are subjects Dunbar-Nelson often explored in her work, including the groundbreaking collections *Violets and Other Tales* and *The Goodness of St. Rocque and Other Stories*. In "The Idler," the speaker observes an idler on the road who dreams all day and yet seems content.

"To be a happy idler, to lounge and sun, And dreaming, pass his long-drawn days away."

NOTES

1 An idle lingerer on the wayside's road,
2 He gathers up his work and yawns away;
3 A little longer, ere the tiresome load
4 Shall be **reduced** to ashes or to clay.

5 No matter if the world has marched along,
6 And scorned his slowness as it quickly passed;
7 No matter, if amid the busy **throng**,
8 He greets some face, **infantile** at the last.

9 His mission? Well, there is but one,
10 And if it is a mission he knows it, nay,
11 To be a happy idler, to lounge and sun,
12 And dreaming, pass his long drawn days away.

13 So dreams he on, his happy life to pass
14 **Content**, without ambitions painful sighs,
15 Until the sands run down into the glass;
16 He smiles—content—unmoved and dies.

17 And yet, with all the pity that you feel
18 For this poor mothling of that flame, the world;
19 Are you the better for your desperate deal,
20 When you, like him, into **infinitude** are hurled?

Alice Ruth Moore Dunbar Nelson

WRITE

DISCUSSION: What is the speaker's opinion of the idler's approach to life? What makes you think so? Support your interpretation with textual evidence. What are your own thoughts about the idler's way of living? Discuss with your classmates what you would want to tell him. Describe any personal experiences that led to your beliefs.

A Cup of Tea

FICTION
Katherine Mansfield
1922

Introduction

Katherine Mansfield (1888–1923) was a Modernist fiction writer from New Zealand who gained widespread recognition after the publication *In a German Pension*, her first collection of short stories. She soon became friends with other famous Modernist writers, such as D.H. Lawrence and Virginia Woolf. The short story "A Cup of Tea" describes a not so typical day in the life of Rosemary Fell, delving into themes of class, gender, beauty, and materialism in London high society.

"'Philip,' she whispered, and she pressed his head against her bosom, 'am I pretty?'"

1   Rosemary Fell was not exactly beautiful. No, you couldn't have called her beautiful. Pretty? Well, if you took her to pieces . . . But why be so cruel as to take anyone to pieces? She was young, brilliant, extremely modern, exquisitely well dressed, amazingly well read in the newest of the new books, and her parties were the most delicious mixture of the really important people and . . . artists—**quaint** creatures, discoveries of hers, some of them too terrifying for words, but others quite presentable and amusing.

Katherine Mansfield

2   Rosemary had been married two years. She had a duck of a boy. No, not Peter—Michael. And her husband absolutely adored her. They were rich, really rich, not just comfortably well off, which is odious and stuffy and sounds like one's grandparents. But if Rosemary wanted to shop she would go to Paris as you and I would go to Bond Street. If she wanted to buy flowers, the car pulled up at that perfect shop in Regent Street, and Rosemary inside the shop just gazed in her dazzled, rather exotic way, and said: "I want those and those and those. Give me four bunches of those. And that jar of roses. Yes, I'll have all the roses in the jar. No, no lilac. I hate lilac. It's got no shape." The attendant bowed and put the lilac out of sight, as though this was only too true; lilac was dreadfully shapeless. "Give me those stumpy little tulips. Those red and white ones." And she was followed to the car by a thin shopgirl staggering under an immense white paper armful that looked like a baby in long clothes . . .

3   One winter afternoon she had been buying something in a little antique shop in Curzon Street. It was a shop she liked. For one thing, one usually had it to oneself. And then the man who kept it was ridiculously fond of serving her. He beamed whenever she came in. He clasped his hands; he was so gratified he could scarcely speak. **Flattery**, of course. All the same, there was something . . .

Reading & Writing Companion

4   "You see, madam," he would explain in his low respectful tones, "I love my things. I would rather not part with them than sell them to someone who does not appreciate them, who has not that fine feeling which is so rare . . ." And, breathing deeply, he unrolled a tiny square of blue velvet and pressed it on the glass counter with his pale finger-tips.

5   To-day it was a little box. He had been keeping it for her. He had shown it to nobody as yet. An exquisite little enamel box with a glaze so fine it looked as though it had been baked in cream. On the lid a minute creature stood under a flowery tree, and a more minute creature still had her arms round his neck. Her hat, really no bigger than a geranium petal, hung from a branch; it had green ribbons. And there was a pink cloud like a watchful cherub floating above their heads. Rosemary took her hands out of her long gloves. She always took off her gloves to examine such things. Yes, she liked it very much. She loved it; it was a great duck. She must have it. And, turning the creamy box, opening and shutting it, she couldn't help noticing how charming her hands were against the blue velvet. The shopman, in some dim cavern of his mind, may have dared to think so too. For he took a pencil, leant over the counter, and his pale, bloodless fingers crept timidly towards those rosy, flashing ones, as he murmured gently: "If I may venture to point out to madam, the flowers on the little lady's bodice."

6   "Charming!" Rosemary admired the flowers. But what was the price? For a moment the shopman did not seem to hear. Then a murmur reached her "Twenty-eight guineas[1], madam."

7   "Twenty-eight guineas." Rosemary gave no sign. She laid the little box down; she buttoned her gloves again. Twenty-eight guineas. Even if one is rich . . . She looked vague. She stared at a plump tea-kettle like a plump hen above the shopman's head, and her voice was dreamy as she answered: "Well, keep it for me – will you? I'll . . ."

8   But the shopman had already bowed as though keeping it for her was all any human being could ask. He would be willing, of course, to keep it for her for ever.

9   The **discreet** door shut with a click. She was outside on the step, gazing at the winter afternoon. Rain was falling, and with the rain it seemed the dark came too, spinning down like ashes. There was a cold bitter taste in the air, and the new-lighted lamps looked sad. Sad were the lights in the houses opposite. Dimly they burned as if regretting something. And people hurried by, hidden under their hateful umbrellas. Rosemary felt a strange pang. She pressed her muff against her breast; she wished she had the little box, too, to

Copyright © BookheadEd Learning, LLC

Skill:
Summarizing

The protagonist, Rosemary is a rich woman on a shopping trip who wants a jewelry box, but leaves it at the shop.

Rosemary doesn't say what's on her mind.

She seems more concerned about how she looks and behaves, than anything else.

1. **guinea** a unit of British currency until the early 19th century

cling to. Of course the car was there. She'd only to cross the pavement. But still she waited. There are moments, horrible moments in life, when one emerges from shelter and looks out, and it's awful. One oughtn't to give way to them. One ought to go home and have an extra-special tea. But at the very instant of thinking that, a young girl, thin, dark, shadowy—where had she come from?—was standing at Rosemary's elbow and a voice like a sigh, almost like a sob, breathed: "Madam, may I speak to you a moment?"

10 "Speak to me?" Rosemary turned. She saw a little battered creature with enormous eyes, someone quite young, no older than herself, who clutched at her coat-collar with reddened hands, and shivered as though she had just come out of the water.

11 "M-madam," stammered the voice. "Would you let me have the price of a cup of tea?"

12 "A cup of tea?" There was something simple, sincere in that voice; it wasn't in the least the voice of a beggar. "Then have you no money at all?" asked Rosemary.

13 "None, madam," came the answer.

14 "How extraordinary!" Rosemary peered through the dusk, and the girl gazed back at her. How more than extraordinary! And suddenly it seemed to Rosemary such an adventure. It was like something out of a novel by Dostoevsky, this meeting in the dusk. Supposing she took the girl home? Supposing she did do one of those things she was always reading about or seeing on the stage, what would happen? It would be thrilling. And she heard herself saying afterwards to the amazement of her friends: "I simply took her home with me," as she stepped forward and said to that dim person beside her: "Come home to tea with me."

15 The girl drew back startled. She even stopped shivering for a moment. Rosemary put out a hand and touched her arm. "I mean it," she said, smiling. And she felt how simple and kind her smile was. "Why won't you? Do. Come home with me now in my car and have tea."

16 "You—you don't mean it, madam," said the girl, and there was pain in her voice.

17 "But I do," cried Rosemary. "I want you to. To please me. Come along."

18 The girl put her fingers to her lips and her eyes devoured Rosemary. "You're—you're not taking me to the police station?" she stammered.

19 "The police station!" Rosemary laughed out. "Why should I be so cruel? No, I only want to make you warm and to hear—anything you care to tell me."

NOTES

20 Hungry people are easily led. The footman held the door of the car open, and a moment later they were skimming through the dusk.

21 "There!" said Rosemary. She had a feeling of triumph as she slipped her hand through the velvet strap. She could have said, "Now I've got you," as she gazed at the little captive she had netted. But of course she meant it kindly. Oh, more than kindly. She was going to prove to this girl that—wonderful things did happen in life, that—fairy godmothers were real, that—rich people had hearts, and that women were sisters. She turned impulsively, saying: "Don't be frightened. After all, why shouldn't you come back with me? We're both women. If I'm the more fortunate, you ought to expect . . ."

22 But happily at that moment, for she didn't know how the sentence was going to end, the car stopped. The bell was rung, the door opened, and with a charming, protecting, almost embracing movement, Rosemary drew the other into the hall. Warmth, softness, light, a sweet scent, all those things so familiar to her she never even thought about them, she watched that other receive. It was fascinating. She was like the rich little girl in her nursery with all the cupboards to open, all the boxes to unpack.

23 "Come, come upstairs," said Rosemary, longing to begin to be generous. "Come up to my room." And, besides, she wanted to spare this poor little thing from being stared at by the servants; she decided as they mounted the stairs she would not even ring for Jeanne, but take off her things by herself. The great thing was to be natural!

24 And "There!" cried Rosemary again, as they reached her beautiful big bedroom with the curtains drawn, the fire leaping on her wonderful lacquer[2] furniture, her gold cushions and the primrose[3] and blue rugs.

25 The girl stood just inside the door; she seemed dazed. But Rosemary didn't mind that.

26 "Come and sit down," she cried, dragging her big chair up to the fire, "in this comfy chair. Come and get warm. You look so dreadfully cold."

27 "I daren't, madam," said the girl, and she edged backwards.

28 "Oh, please,"—Rosemary ran forward—"you mustn't be frightened, you mustn't, really. Sit down, when I've taken off my things we shall go into the next room and have tea and be cosy. Why are you afraid?" And gently she half pushed the thin figure into its deep cradle.

Skill:
Word Patterns and Relationships

I infer that the -ed at the ending indicates mounted is a verb.

The word might have something to do with climbing because the word sounds like "mountain," and that would make sense given the context.

---

2. **lacquer** a liquid used to make wood shiny
3. **primrose** a European flowering plant that produces flowers with small yellow petals

29 But there was no answer. The girl stayed just as she had been put, with her hands by her sides and her mouth slightly open. To be quite sincere, she looked rather stupid. But Rosemary wouldn't acknowledge it. She leant over her, saying: "Won't you take off your hat? Your pretty hair is all wet. And one is so much more comfortable without a hat, isn't one?"

30 There was a whisper that sounded like "Very good, madam," and the crushed hat was taken off.

31 "And let me help you off with your coat, too," said Rosemary.

32 The girl stood up. But she held onto the chair with one hand and let Rosemary pull. It was quite an effort. The other scarcely helped her at all. She seemed to stagger like a child, and the thought came and went through Rosemary's mind, that if people wanted helping they must respond a little, just a little, otherwise it became very difficult indeed. And what was she to do with the coat now? She left it on the floor, and the hat too. She was just going to take a cigarette off the mantelpiece when the girl said quickly, but so lightly and strangely: "I'm very sorry, madam, but I'm going to faint. I shall go off, madam, if I don't have something."

33 "Good heavens, how thoughtless I am!" Rosemary rushed to the bell.

34 "Tea! Tea at once! And some brandy immediately!"

35 The maid was gone again, but the girl almost cried out: "No, I don't want no brandy. I never drink brandy. It's a cup of tea I want, madam." And she burst into tears.

36 It was a terrible and fascinating moment. Rosemary knelt beside her chair.

37 "Don't cry, poor little thing," she said. "Don't cry." And she gave the other her lace handkerchief. She really was touched beyond words. She put her arm round those thin, bird-like shoulders.

38 Now at last the other forgot to be shy, forgot everything except that they were both women, and gasped out: "I can't go on no longer like this. I can't bear it. I can't bear it. I shall do away with myself. I can't bear no more."

39 "You shan't have to. I'll look after you. Don't cry any more. Don't you see what a good thing it was that you met me? We'll have tea and you'll tell me everything. And I shall arrange something. I promise. Do stop crying. It's so exhausting. Please!"

40 The other did stop just in time for Rosemary to get up before the tea came. She had the table placed between them. She plied the poor little creature

with everything, all the sandwiches, all the bread and butter, and every time her cup was empty she filled it with tea, cream and sugar. People always said sugar was so nourishing. As for herself she didn't eat; she smoked and looked away tactfully so that the other should not be shy.

41 And really the effect of that slight meal was marvelous. When the tea-table was carried away a new being, a light, frail creature with tangled hair, dark lips, deep, lighted eyes, lay back in the big chair in a kind of sweet **languor**, looking at the blaze. Rosemary lit a fresh cigarette; it was time to begin.

42 "And when did you have your last meal?" she asked softly.

43 But at that moment the door-handle turned.

44 "Rosemary, may I come in?" It was Philip.

45 "Of course."

46 He came in. "Oh, I'm so sorry," he said, and stopped and stared.

47 "It's quite all right," said Rosemary, smiling. "This is my friend, Miss—"

48 "Smith, madam," said the languid figure, who was strangely still and unafraid.

49 "Smith," said Rosemary. "We are going to have a little talk."

50 "Oh yes," said Philip. "Quite," and his eye caught sight of the coat and hat on the floor. He came over to the fire and turned his back to it. "It's a beastly afternoon," he said curiously, still looking at that **listless** figure, looking at its hands and boots, and then at Rosemary again.

51 "Yes, isn't it?" said Rosemary enthusiastically. "Vile."

52 Philip smiled his charming smile. "As a matter of fact," said he, "I wanted you to come into the library for a moment. Would you? Will Miss Smith excuse us?"

53 The big eyes were raised to him, but Rosemary answered for her: "Of course she will." And they went out of the room together.

54 "I say," said Philip, when they were alone. "Explain. Who is she? What does it all mean?"

55 Rosemary, laughing, leaned against the door and said: "I picked her up in Curzon Street. Really. She's a real pick-up. She asked me for the price of a cup of tea, and I brought her home with me."

56 "But what on earth are you going to do with her?" cried Philip.

57 "Be nice to her," said Rosemary quickly. "Be frightfully nice to her. Look after her. I don't know how. We haven't talked yet. But show her—treat her—make her feel—"

58 "My darling girl," said Philip, "you're quite mad, you know. It simply can't be done."

59 "I knew you'd say that," retorted Rosemary. "Why not? I want to. Isn't that a reason? And besides, one's always reading about these things. I decided—"

60 "But," said Philip slowly, and he cut the end of a cigar, "she's so astonishingly pretty."

61 "Pretty?" Rosemary was so surprised that she blushed. "Do you think so? I—I hadn't thought about it."

62 "Good Lord!" Philip struck a match. "She's absolutely lovely. Look again, my child. I was bowled over when I came into your room just now. However . . . I think you're making a ghastly mistake. Sorry, darling, if I'm **crude** and all that. But let me know if Miss Smith is going to dine with us in time for me to look up *The Milliner's Gazette*[4]."

63 "You absurd creature!" said Rosemary, and she went out of the library, but not back to her bedroom. She went to her writing-room and sat down at her desk. Pretty! Absolutely lovely! Bowled over! Her heart beat like a heavy bell. Pretty! Lovely! She drew her cheque-book towards her. But no, cheques would be no use, of course. She opened a drawer and took out five pound notes, looked at them, put two back, and holding the three squeezed in her hand, she went back to her bedroom.

64 Half an hour later Philip was still in the library, when Rosemary came in.

65 "I only wanted to tell you," said she, and she leaned against the door again and looked at him with her dazzled exotic gaze, "Miss Smith won't dine with us to-night."

66 Philip put down the paper. "Oh, what's happened? Previous engagement?"

67 Rosemary came over and sat down on his knee. "She insisted on going," said she, "so I gave the poor little thing a present of money. I couldn't keep her against her will, could I?" she added softly.

4. ***The Milliner's Gazette*** Hill's Milliner's Gazette was a trade paper published in London for hatmakers, an occupation associated with prostitution

68   Rosemary had just done her hair, darkened her eyes a little and put on her pearls. She put up her hands and touched Philip's cheeks.

69   "Do you like me?" said she, and her tone, sweet, husky, troubled him.

70   "I like you awfully," he said, and he held her tighter. "Kiss me."

71   There was a pause.

72   Then Rosemary said dreamily: "I saw a fascinating little box to-day. It cost twenty-eight guineas. May I have it?"

73   Philip jumped her on his knee. "You may, little wasteful one," said he.

74   But that was not really what Rosemary wanted to say.

75   "Philip," she whispered, and she pressed his head against her bosom, "am I *pretty*?"

Skill:
Summarizing

Rosemary directs her husband's attention to her, and away from the girl. She seems insecure.

At the end of the story, Rosemary returns to what she really wanted all along.

First Read

Read "A Cup of Tea." After you read, complete the Think Questions below.

THINK QUESTIONS

1. Why does Rosemary want to take the girl from the street home with her? Is it really just to offer her a cup of tea? Cite evidence from the text to support your answer.

2. Why does Rosemary like the enamel box she discovers at the antique shop? Cite evidence from the text to support your answer.

3. How does Rosemary react when Philip comments that the girl Rosemary brought home is "astonishingly pretty"? Why does she react this way? Cite evidence from the text to support your answer.

4. Which context clues helped you determine the meaning of the word **discreet** as it is used in the text? Write your definition of *discreet* here, and indicate which clues helped you figure out the meaning of the word.

5. The Latin word *crudus* means "raw or rough." With this in mind, write your best definition of the word **crude** as it is used in the text. Indicate which context clues helped you determine the word's meaning.

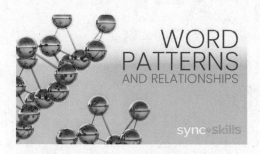

Skill: Word Patterns and Relationships

Use the Checklist to analyze Word Patterns and Relationships in "A Cup of Tea." Refer to the sample student annotations about Word Patterns and Relationships in the text.

••• CHECKLIST FOR WORD PATTERNS AND RELATIONSHIPS

In order to identify patterns of word changes to indicate different meanings or parts of speech, do the following:

- ✓ determine the word's part of speech

- ✓ when reading, use context clues to make a preliminary determination of the meaning of the word

- ✓ when writing a response to a text, check that you understand the meaning and part of speech and that it makes sense in your sentence

- ✓ consult a dictionary to verify your preliminary determination of the meanings and parts of speech

- ✓ be sure to read all of the definitions, and then decide which definition, form, and part of speech makes sense within the context of the text

To identify and correctly use patterns of word changes that indicate different meanings or parts of speech, consider the following questions:

- ✓ What is the intended meaning of the word?

- ✓ Do I know that this word form is the correct part of speech? Do I understand the word patterns for this particular word?

- ✓ When I consult a dictionary, can I confirm that the meaning I have determined for this word is correct? Do I know how to use it correctly?

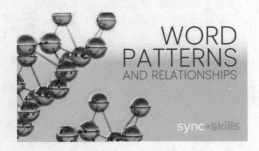

Skill: Word Patterns and Relationships

Reread paragraph 21 of "A Cup of Tea." Then, using the Checklist on the previous page, answer the multiple-choice questions below.

⟳ YOUR TURN

1. What part of speech is "impulsively"?

   ○ A. noun
   ○ B. verb
   ○ C. adjective
   ○ D. adverb

2. Given the definitions provided, what is most likely the meaning of *impulsively*?

   Impulsive
   /ɪmˈpʌlsɪv/
   noun
   1. act in the moment
   2. related to electrical energy
   3. a force

   ○ A. To cause electrical energy
   ○ B. To act without thinking
   ○ C. To perform actions without one's consent
   ○ D. To consider the consequences well in advance

Skill:
Summarizing

Use the Checklist to analyze Summarizing in "A Cup of Tea." Refer to the sample student annotations about Summarizing in the text.

In order to determine how to write an objective summary of a text, note the following:

✓ answers to the basic questions *who, what, where, when, why,* and *how*

✓ in literature or nonfiction, note how two or more themes or central ideas are developed over the course of the text, and how they interact and build on one another to produce a complex account

✓ stay objective, and do not add your own personal thoughts, judgments, or opinions to the summary

To provide an objective summary of a text, consider the following questions:

✓ What are the answers to basic *who, what, where, when, why,* and *how* questions in literature and works of nonfiction?

✓ Does my summary include how two or more themes or central ideas are developed over the course of the text, and how they interact and build on one another in my summary?

✓ Is my summary objective, or have I added my own thoughts, judgments, and personal opinions?

Please note that excerpts and passages in the StudySync® library and this workbook are intended as touchstones to generate interest in an author's work. The excerpts and passages do not substitute for the reading of entire texts, and StudySync® strongly recommends that students seek out and purchase the whole literary or informational work in order to experience it as the author intended. Links to online resellers are available in our digital library. In addition, complete works may be ordered through an authorized reseller by filling out and returning to StudySync® the order form enclosed in this workbook.

Reading & Writing Companion   41

Skill:
Summarizing

Reread paragraphs 9–13 of "A Cup of Tea." Then, using the Checklist on the previous page, answer the multiple-choice questions below.

⟳ YOUR TURN

1. The following is a sentence that a student wrote to summarize this passage of the text. What feedback would you give to help improve this summary?

> "Rosemary feels sad because she can't afford the antique she feels she is entitled to, when a young girl approaches her in the street."

- ○ A. The summary of the passage is incomplete because it does not mention the "extra-special tea."
- ○ B. The summary does not provide basic information, such as Rosemary's last name or where she is shopping.
- ○ C. This is an analysis, not an objective summary, because the text does not explicitly say that Rosemary is sad.
- ○ D. The summary is not objective because the word "entitled" has negative connotations, and this is not implied in the passage.

2. If you were to write a summary of this passage, what two themes do you notice are repeated in this paragraph?

- ○ A. Having too much wealth and being lonely
- ○ B. Being homesick and knowing where you belong
- ○ C. Isolation in one's own world and dissatisfaction
- ○ D. The wealthy are hypocritical and insecurity

Close Read

Reread "A Cup of Tea." As you reread, complete the Skills Focus questions below. Then use your answers and annotations from the questions to help you complete the Write activity.

🎯 SKILLS FOCUS

1. Reread paragraph 48. Highlight the word *languid*, and, in your annotation, use your knowledge of word patterns and relationships to answer the following questions: What part of speech is this word? How do you know? What do you think this word means and why?

2. Identify details about the economic setting that contrast Rosemary's wealth and Miss Smith's poverty, and explain why it might be important to include these details in a summary of the story.

3. Identify a passage that shows Rosemary has conflicting feelings toward Miss Smith, and explain how these feelings contribute to the theme of materialism among the upper classes.

4. Identify a comment Philip makes about Miss Smith's beauty and in brief summary explain two possible reasons why Philip discourages his wife from helping Miss Smith.

5. This story revolves around the character of Rosemary as she seeks a connection with someone or something. What details in the story help you understand why Rosemary might feel so alienated? What about her life has caused this?

✏️ WRITE

COMPARE AND CONTRAST: Write a response in which you compare and contrast the ideas and attitudes expressed about wealth and poverty in "miss rosie," "The Idler," and "A Cup of Tea." Remember to use textual evidence from "A Cup of Tea" to support your response.

The Glass Menagerie

DRAMA
Tennessee Williams
1944

Introduction

Thomas Lanier ("Tennessee") Williams III was one of America's most influential 20th century playwrights, and it was his semi-autobiographical work *The Glass Menagerie* that launched him to fame after years of obscurity. Here, in the fifth scene from the play, frustrated would-be poet Tom Wingfield responds to his mother Amanda's inquiries about the gentleman caller he has invited over to meet Laura, his painfully shy younger sister.

"A fire escape landing's a poor excuse for a porch."

SCENE FIVE

 NOTES

1 *Legend on the screen:* "**Annunciation**."

2 *Music is heard as the light slowly comes on.*

3 *It is early dusk of a spring evening. Supper has just been finished in the Wingfield apartment. Amanda and Laura, in light-colored dresses, are removing dishes from the table in the dining room, which is shadowy, their movements formalized almost as a dance or ritual, their moving forms as pale and silent as moths. Tom, in white shirt and trousers, rises from the table and crosses toward the fire escape.*

4 AMANDA [*as he passes her*]: Son, will you do me a favor?

5 TOM: What?

6 AMANDA: Comb your hair! You look so pretty when your hair is combed!

7 [*Tom slouches on the sofa with the evening paper. Its enormous headline reads: "Franco Triumphs[1]."*]

8 There is only one respect in which I would like you to **emulate** your father.

9 TOM: What respect is that?

10 AMANDA: The care he always took of his appearance. He never allowed himself to look untidy.

11 [*He throws down the paper and crosses to the fire escape.*]

12 Where are you going?

---

1. **Franco Triumphs** eventual Spanish dictator Francisco Franco fought for the Nationalists in the Spanish Civil War, who were eventually victorious and installed him as leader from 1939 to 1975.

13　TOM: I'm going out to smoke.

14　AMANDA: You smoke too much. A pack a day at fifteen cents a pack. How much would that amount to in a month? Thirty times fifteen is how much, Tom? Figure it out and you will be astounded at what you could save. Enough to give you a night-school course in accounting at Washington U.! Just think what a wonderful thing that would be for you, son!

15　[*Tom is unmoved by the thought.*]

16　TOM: I'd rather smoke. [*He steps out on the landing, letting the screen door slam.*]

17　AMANDA [*sharply*]: I know! That's the tragedy of it. . . . [*Alone, she turns to look at her husband's picture.*]

18　[*Dance music: "The World Is Waiting for the Sunrise!"*]

**Skill:
Media**

The radio play is immediately different from the script: Tom's soliloquy sets the scene, and there is no stage direction or dialogue before it.

Tom sounds different than I imagined. He is more casual in the radio version.

19　TOM [*to the audience*]: Across the alley from us was the Paradise Dance Hall. On evenings in spring the windows and doors were open and the music came outdoors. Sometimes the lights were turned out except for a large glass sphere that the hung from the ceiling. It would turn slowly about and filter the dusk with delicate rainbow colors. Then the orchestra played a waltz or a tango, something that had a slow and sensuous rhythm. Couples would come outside, to the relative privacy of the alley. You could see them kissing behind ash pits and telephone poles. This was the compensation for lives that passed like mine, without any change or adventure. Adventure and change were imminent this year. They were waiting around the corner for all these kids. Suspended in the mist over Berchtesgaden[2], caught in the folds of Chamberlain's umbrella[3]. In Spain there was Guernica![4] But here there was only hot swing music and liquor, dance halls, bars, and movies, and sex that hung in the gloom like a chandelier and flooded the world with brief, deceptive rainbows. . . . All the world was waiting for bombardments!

**Skill:
Dramatic Elements and Structure**

Amanda is clearly out of place in this city. The stage directions provide needed clues about who she is as a character and reveal that she is not at home in the city setting.

20　[*Amanda turns from the picture and comes outside.*]

21　AMANDA [*sighing*]; A fire escape landing's a poor excuse for a porch. [*She spreads a newspaper on a step and sits down, gracefully and demurely as if she were settling into a swing on a Mississippi veranda.*] What are you looking at?

2. **Berchtesgaden** a small German town in the Alps
3. **Chamberlain's umbrella** a figure of speech used to describe England's prime minister Neville Chamberlain's failure to appease Hitler at the Munich Conference in 1938
4. **Guernica** a large oil painting by Pablo Picasso depicting the bombing of the Spanish town of Guernica during the Spanish Civil War

 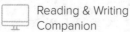

22 TOM: The moon.

23 AMANDA: Is there a moon this evening?

24 TOM: It's rising over Garfinkel's Delicatessen.

25 AMANDA: So it is! A little silver slipper of a moon. Have you made a wish on it yet?

26 TOM: Um-hum.

27 AMANDA: What did you wish for?

28 TOM: That's a secret.

29 AMANDA: A secret, huh? Well, I won't tell mine either. I will be just as mysterious as you.

30 TOM: I bet I can guess what yours is.

31 AMANDA: Is my head so transparent?

32 TOM: You're not a **sphinx**.

33 AMANDA. No, I don't have secrets. I'll tell you what I wished for on the moon. Success and happiness for my precious children! I wish for that whenever there's a moon, and when there isn't a moon, I wish for it, too.

34 TOM: I thought perhaps you wished for a gentleman caller.

35 AMANDA: Why do you say that?

36 TOM: Don't you remember asking me to fetch one?

37 AMANDA: I remember suggesting that it would be nice for your sister if you brought home some nice young man from the warehouse. I think that I've made that suggestion more than once.

38 TOM: Yes, you have made it repeatedly.

39 AMANDA: Well?

40 TOM: We are going to have one.

41 AMANDA: *What?*

Skill:
Media

The audiobook is more similar to the script. The actor changes his voice to play the characters. But it sounds unnatural when he says "Um-hum", perhaps because this interpretation is meant to be an exact reading of the script.

Please note that excerpts and passages in the StudySync® library and this workbook are intended as touchstones to generate interest in an author's work. The excerpts and passages do not substitute for the reading of entire texts, and StudySync® strongly recommends that students seek out and purchase the whole literary or informational work in order to experience it as the author intended. Links to online resellers are available in our digital library. In addition, complete works may be ordered through an authorized reseller by filling out and returning to StudySync® the order form enclosed in this workbook.

Reading & Writing Companion   **47**

42   TOM: A gentleman caller!

43   [*The annunciation is celebrated with music.*]

44   [*Amanda rises.*]

45   [*Image on screen:* A caller with a bouquet.]

46   AMANDA: You mean you have asked some nice young man to come over?

47   TOM: Yep. I've asked him to dinner.

48   AMANDA: You really did?

49   TOM: I did!

50   AMANDA: You did, and did he—*accept?*

51   TOM: He did!

52   AMANDA: Well, well—well, well! That's—lovely!

53   TOM: I thought that you would be pleased.

54   AMANDA: It's definite then?

55   TOM: Very definite.

56   AMANDA: Soon?

57   TOM: Very soon.

Skill:
Media

Amanda is stuttering, which is not in the script. This is the actor's interpretation. In the script, I thought she seemed more accusatory than nervous. Nervousness might be easier to communicate over the radio.

58   AMANDA: For heaven's sake, stop putting on and tell me some things, will you?

59   TOM: What things do you want me to tell you?

60   AMANDA: *Naturally* I would like to know when he's *coming*!

61   TOM: He's coming tomorrow.

62   AMANDA: *Tomorrow?*

63   TOM: Yep. Tomorrow.

64   AMANDA: But, Tom!

Copyright © BookheadEd Learning, LLC

65 TOM: Yes, Mother?

66 AMANDA: Tomorrow gives me no time!

67 TOM: Time for what?

68 AMANDA: Preparations! Why didn't you phone me at once, as soon as you asked him, the minute that he accepted? Then, don't you see, I could have been getting ready!

69 TOM: You don't have to make any fuss.

70 AMANDA: Oh, Tom, Tom, Tom, of course I have to make a fuss! I want things nice, not sloppy! Not thrown together. I'll certainly have to do some fast thinking, won't I?

71 TOM: I don't see why you have to think at all.

72 AMANDA: You just don't know. We can't have a gentleman caller in a pigsty! All my wedding silver has to be polished, the monogrammed table linen ought to be laundered! The windows have to be washed and fresh curtains put up. And how about clothes? We have to *wear* something, don't we?

73 TOM: Mother, this boy is no one to make a fuss over!

74 AMANDA: Do you realize he's the first young man we've introduced to your sister? It's terrible, dreadful, disgraceful that poor little sister has never received a single gentleman caller! Tom, come inside! [*She opens the screen door.*]

75 TOM: What for?

76 AMANDA: I want to ask you some things.

77 TOM: If you're going to make such a fuss, I'll call it off, I'll tell him not to come!

78 AMANDA: You certainly won't do anything of the kind. Nothing offends people worse than broken engagements. It simply means I'll have to work like a Turk! We won't be brilliant, but we will pass inspection. Come on inside.

79 [*Tom follows her inside, groaning.*]

80 Sit down.

81 TOM: Any particular place you would like me to sit?

82   AMANDA: Thank heavens I've got that new sofa! I'm also making payments on a floor lamp I'll have sent out! And put the chintz covers on, they'll brighten things up! Of course I'd hoped to have these walls re-papered. . . . What is the young man's name?

83   TOM: His name is O'Connor.

84   AMANDA: That, of course, means fish—tomorrow is Friday! I'll have that salmon loaf—with Durkee's dressing! What does he do? He works at the warehouse?

85   TOM: Of course! How else would I—

86   AMANDA: Tom, he—doesn't drink?

87   TOM: Why do you ask me that?

88   AMANDA: Your father *did!*

89   TOM: Don't get started on that!

90   AMANDA: He *does* drink, then?

91   TOM: Not that I know of!

92   AMANDA: Make sure, be certain! The last thing I want for my daughter's a boy who drinks!

93   TOM: Aren't you being a little premature? Mr. O'Connor has not yet appeared on the scene!

94   AMANDA: But will tomorrow. To meet your sister, and what do I know about his character? Nothing! Old maids are better off than wives of drunkards!

95   TOM: Oh, my God!

96   AMANDA: Be still!

97   TOM: [*leaning forward to whisper*]: Lots of fellows meet girls whom they don't marry!

98   AMANDA: Oh, talk sensibly, Tom—and don't be sarcastic! [*She has gotten a hairbrush.*]

99   TOM: What are you doing?

NOTES

100 AMANDA: I'm brushing that cowlick down! [*She attacks his hair with the brush.*] What is this young man's position at the warehouse?

101 TOM [*submitting grimly to the brush and interrogation*]: This young man's position is that of a shipping clerk, Mother.

102 AMANDA: Sounds to me like a fairly responsible job, the sort of a job *you* would be in if you had more *get-up*. What is his salary? Have you any idea?

103 TOM: I would judge it to be approximately eighty-five dollars a month.

104 AMANDA: Well—not princely, but—

105 TOM: Twenty more than I make.

106 AMANDA: Yes, how well I know! But for a family man, eighty-five dollars a month is not much more than you can just get by on. . . .

107 TOM: Yes, but Mr. O'Connor is not a family man.

108 AMANDA: He might be, mightn't he? Some time in the future?

109 TOM: I see. Plans and provisions.

110 AMANDA: You are the only young man that I know of who ignores the fact that the future becomes the present, the present the past, and the past turns into everlasting regret if you don't plan for it!

111 TOM: I will think that over and see what I can make of it.

112 AMANDA: Don't be **supercilious** with your mother! Tell me some more about this—what do you call him?

113 TOM: James D. O'Connor. The D. is for Delaney.

114 AMANDA: Irish on *both* sides! *Gracious!* And doesn't drink?

115 TOM: Shall I call him up and ask him right this minute?

116 AMANDA: The only way to find out about those things is to make discreet inquiries at the proper moment. When I was a girl in Blue Mountain and it was suspected that a young man drank, the girl whose attentions he had been receiving, if any girl *was*, would sometimes speak to the minister of his church, or rather her father would if her father was living, and sort of feel him out on the young man's character. That is the way such things are discreetly handled to keep a young woman from making a tragic mistake!

Please note that excerpts and passages in the StudySync® library and this workbook are intended as touchstones to generate interest in an author's work. The excerpts and passages do not substitute for the reading of entire texts, and StudySync® strongly recommends that students seek out and purchase the whole literary or informational work in order to experience it as the author intended. Links to online resellers are available in our digital library. In addition, complete works may be ordered through an authorized reseller by filling out and returning to StudySync® the order form enclosed in this workbook.

Reading & Writing Companion

51

117   TOM: Then how did you happen to make a tragic mistake?

118   AMANDA: That innocent look of your father's had everyone fooled! He *smiled*—the world was *enchanted!* No girl can do worse than put herself at the mercy of a handsome appearance! I hope that Mr. O'Connor is not too good-looking.

119   TOM: No, he's not too good-looking. He's covered with freckles and hasn't too much of a nose.

120   AMANDA: He's not right-down **homely**, though?

121   TOM: Not right-down homely. Just medium homely, I'd say.

122   AMANDA: Character's what to look for in a man.

123   TOM: That's what I've always said, Mother.

124   AMANDA: You've never said anything of the kind and I suspect you would never give it a thought.

125   TOM: Don't be so suspicious of me.

126   AMANDA: At least I hope he's the type that's up and coming.

127   TOM: I think he really goes in for self-improvement.

128   AMANDA: What reason have you to think so?

129   TOM: He goes to night school.

130   AMANDA: [*beaming*]: Splendid! What does he do, I mean study?

131   TOM: Radio engineering and public speaking!

132   AMANDA: Then he has visions of being advanced in the world! Any young man who studies public speaking is aiming to have an executive job some day! And radio engineering? A thing for the future! Both of these facts are very illuminating. Those are the sort of things that a mother should know concerning any young man who comes to call on her daughter. Seriously or—not.

133   TOM: One little warning. He doesn't know about Laura. I didn't let on that we had dark ulterior motives. I just said, why don't you come and have dinner with us? He said okay and that was the whole conversation.

Skill:
Dramatic Elements
and Structure

Was Tom worried James would not come to dinner if he knew about his sister? Or does he really think these are "dark ulterior motives"?

Amanda makes fun of Tom in a kind way by calling him eloquent as an oyster.

---

134   AMANDA: I bet it was! You're eloquent as an oyster. However, he'll know about Laura when he gets here. When he sees how lovely and sweet and pretty she is, he'll thank his lucky stars he was asked to dinner.

135   TOM: Mother, you mustn't expect too much of Laura.

136   AMANDA: What do you mean?

137   TOM: Laura seems all those things to you and me because she's ours and we love her. We don't even notice she's crippled any more.

138   AMANDA: Don't say crippled! You know that I never allow that word to be used!

139   TOM: But face facts, Mother. She is and—that's not all—

140   AMANDA: What do you mean "not all"?

141   TOM: Laura is very different from other girls.

142   AMANDA: I think the difference is all to her advantage.

143   TOM: Not quite all—in the eyes of others—strangers—she's terribly shy and lives in a world of her own and those things make her seem a little peculiar to people outside the house.

144   AMANDA: Don't say peculiar.

145   TOM: Face the facts. She is.

146   [*The dance hall music changes to a tango that has a minor and somewhat ominous tone.*]

147   AMANDA: In what way is she peculiar—may I ask?

148   TOM [*gently*]: She lives in a world of her own—a world of little glass ornaments, Mother. . . .

149   [*He gets up. Amanda remains holding the brush, looking at him, troubled.*]

150   She plays old phonograph records and—that's about all—

151   [*He glances at himself in the mirror and crosses to the door.*]

152   AMANDA [*sharply*]: Where are you going?

Please note that excerpts and passages in the StudySync® library and this workbook are intended as touchstones to generate interest in an author's work. The excerpts and passages do not substitute for the reading of entire texts, and StudySync® strongly recommends that students seek out and purchase the whole literary or informational work in order to experience it as the author intended. Links to online resellers are available in our digital library. In addition, complete works may be ordered through an authorized reseller by filling out and returning to StudySync® the order form enclosed in this workbook.

Reading & Writing
Companion   53

153 TOM: I'm going to the movies. [*He goes out the screen door.*]

154 AMANDA: Not to the movies, every night to the movies! [*She follows quickly to the screen door.*] I don't believe you always go to the movies!

155 [*He is gone. Amanda look worriedly after him for a moment. Then vitality and optimism return and she turns from the door, crossing to the portieres.*]

156 Laura! Laura!

157 [*Laura answers from the kitchenette.*]

158 LAURA: Yes, Mother.

159 AMANDA: Let those dishes go and come in front!

160 [*Laura appears with a dish towel. Amanda speaks to her gaily.*]

161 Laura, come here and make a wish on the moon!

162 [*Screen image:* The Moon.]

163 LAURA [*entering*]: Moon—moon?

164 AMANDA: A little silver slipper of a moon. Look over your left shoulder, Laura, and make a wish!

165 [*Laura looks faintly puzzled as if called out of sleep. Amanda seizes her shoulders and turns her at an angle by the door.*]

166 Now! Now, darling, *wish!*

167 LAURA: What shall I wish for, Mother?

168 AMANDA [*her voice trembling and her eyes suddenly filling with tears*]: Happiness! Good fortune!

169 [*The sound of the violin rises and the stage dims out.*]

The Glass Menagerie by Tennessee Williams. Copyright © 1945, renewed 1973 The University of the South. Reprinted by permission of Georges Borchardt, Inc. for the Estate of Tennessee Williams.

First Read

Read *The Glass Menagerie*. After you read, complete the Think Questions below.

 THINK QUESTIONS

1. What does Tom remember as he steps out onto the fire escape? Describe his memories using details from the text. What does this memory suggest about his feelings about his own life at that moment? Support your inference with a quotation from the text.

2. What ideas or feelings does the moon inspire in Amanda? What can you infer about Amanda based on the wish she expresses when seeing the moon and her behavior throughout this scene? Cite details from the text to support your inferences.

3. How does Amanda react when Tom reveals that he has invited a "gentleman caller" to dinner? What sorts of qualities does she ask about? What does her reaction suggest about her character and her relationship to her children? Support your answer with textual evidence.

4. Use context to determine the meaning of the word **emulate** as it is used in *The Glass Menagerie*. Write your definition of "emulate" here and tell how you found it.

5. Use context to determine the meaning of the word **homely** as it is used in *The Glass Menagerie*. Write your definition of "homely" here and tell how you found it.

Please note that excerpts and passages in the StudySync® library and this workbook are intended as touchstones to generate interest in an author's work. The excerpts and passages do not substitute for the reading of entire texts, and StudySync® strongly recommends that students seek out and purchase the whole literary or informational work in order to experience it as the author intended. Links to online resellers are available in our digital library. In addition, complete works may be ordered through an authorized reseller by filling out and returning to StudySync® the order form enclosed in this workbook.

Reading & Writing Companion

55

Skill: Dramatic Elements and Structure

Use the Checklist to analyze Dramatic Elements and Structure in "The Glass Menagerie." Refer to the sample student annotations about Dramatic Elements and Structure in the text.

••• CHECKLIST FOR DRAMATIC ELEMENTS AND STRUCTURE

In order to determine the author's choices regarding the development of a drama, note the following:

- ✓ how character choices and dialogue affect the plot

- ✓ the stage directions and how they are used to reveal character and plot development

- ✓ the names of all the characters, and their relationships with one another

- ✓ character development, including personality traits, motivations, decisions they make, and actions they take

- ✓ the setting(s) of the story and how it influences the characters and the events of the plot

To analyze the impact of the author's choices regarding how to develop and relate elements of a story or drama, consider the following questions:

- ✓ How does the setting affect the characters and plot?

- ✓ How do the characters' actions help develop the theme or message of the play?

- ✓ How does the order of events in the play affect the development of the drama?

- ✓ How do the choices the characters make help advance the plot?

Skill: Dramatic Elements and Structure

Reread paragraphs 152–169 of *The Glass Menagerie*. Then, using the Checklist on the previous page, answer the multiple-choice questions below.

YOUR TURN

1. What is the most likely reason that Laura is introduced at the end of the scene?

   ○ A. To show how dialogue between Laura and Amanda differs from conversations that Amanda had with Tom.

   ○ B. To allow the audience to finally see Laura and determine why Tom and Amanda seem so worried about her.

   ○ C. To provide details about Laura's personality traits to the audience that show how wrong Tom and Amanda are about her.

   ○ D. To reinforce the relationship between mother and daughter, and show that Tom is the outcast of the family.

2. Which of the following best describes the effect of the final stage direction in this scene?

   ○ A. It uses music to add a specific emotion to the closing dialogue in the scene.

   ○ B. It provides resolution to the scene through the character's actions.

   ○ C. It provides background music and necessary information to the audience.

   ○ D. It uses music to create tension so the audience wants to know what happens next.

Skill: Media

Use the Checklist to analyze Media in *The Glass Menagerie*. Refer to the sample student annotations about Media in the text.

••• CHECKLIST FOR MEDIA

In order to identify multiple interpretations of a story, drama, or poem, do the following:

- ✓ note the similarities and differences in different media, such as the live production of a play or a recorded novel or poetry

- ✓ evaluate how each version interprets the source text

- ✓ consider how, within the same medium, a story can have multiple interpretations if told by writers from different time periods and cultures

- ✓ consider how stories told in the same medium will likely reflect the specific objectives as well as the respective ideas, concerns, and values of each writer

To analyze multiple interpretations of a story, drama, or poem, evaluating how each version interprets the source text, consider the following questions:

- ✓ What medium is being used, and how does it affect the interpretation of the source text?

- ✓ What are the main similarities and differences between the two (or more) versions?

- ✓ If each version is from a different time period and/or culture, what does each version reveal about the author's objectives and the time period and culture in which it was written?

Skill:
Media

Reread lines 97–114 of *The Glass Menagerie* and review the radio and audiobook clips in the digital lesson. Then, using the Checklist on the previous page, answer the multiple-choice questions below.

⟳ YOUR TURN

1. What is the most likely reason that the audiobook reads some stage directions from this passage and not others?

   ○ A. Some stage directions were removed due to time constraints in the audiobook version of the play.

   ○ B. Each interpretation varies given the time period and culture, and stage directions are less popular in 2018.

   ○ C. The stage directions are read only when the audience of the audiobook version needs the additional information.

   ○ D. The playwright omitted some stage directions because the actors did not need the instructions in the audiobook version.

2. In what way is the first line in this clip from the 1951 radio play different from the script?

   ○ A. The radio play removes the reference to marriage that is included in the script.

   ○ B. The radio play does not use the original words from the script in the first line.

   ○ C. The actor does not whisper as instructed by the stage direction.

   ○ D. The actor is devoid of emotion, unlike instructions in the script.

3. What is one effect of having a live studio audience for the radio play?

   ○ A. The live studio audience reaction influences the actor's interpretation of the play.

   ○ B. The playwright adjusts the script to accomodate for the audience reaction.

   ○ C. The live studio audience sees the stage directions in action and tell the listener what is happening.

   ○ D. The actors occasionally have to pause for the laughter to subside so that they can be heard.

Close Read

Reread *The Glass Menagerie*. As you reread, complete the Skills Focus questions below. Then use your answers and annotations from the questions to help you complete the Write activity.

◎ SKILLS FOCUS

1. Reread the stage directions. How do music and lighting cues contribute to the text? How do they affect your understanding of what happens in the scene and why the events are important to the story? Highlight textual evidence and make annotations to explain your choices.

2. In this scene, Williams offers indirect characterization of Laura through dialogue between Amanda and Tom. What can readers infer about Laura based on their descriptions? How do Laura's actions at the end of the scene compare and contrast with readers' expectations? Support your answer with textual evidence and make annotations to explain your answer choices.

3. Identify places in the text where Amanda shows concern about appearances. What sorts of things is she worried about and why? How does her portrayal in the radio play and in the audio book reflect the character's perspective on the importance of appearances? Highlight textual evidence and make annotations to support your explanation.

4. Compare and contrast the portrayals of Tom in the radio play and in the audiobook. How do the actors' portrayals compare to your first impressions of Tom in Williams's original text? Highlight your textual evidence and make annotations to explain your choices.

5. *The Glass Menagerie* is a "memory play" loosely based on Williams's own experiences with his mother and sister. How does the character of Tom represent feelings of alienation? What might be causing those feelings? Highlight textual evidence and make annotations to explain your ideas.

✏ WRITE

COMPARE AND CONTRAST: Listen to the audio clips of *The Glass Menagerie*. How do these two versions differ from each other? How does each version interpret the source text of the play, making the dramatic elements work for that specific medium? Choose at least one substantial difference between the two versions, and explain and evaluate how each version interprets the source material. Support your writing with textual evidence and both audio recordings.

A Room Of One's Own

ARGUMENTATIVE TEXT
Virginia Woolf
1929

Introduction

Virginia Woolf (1882–1941) was one of the most important Modernist authors of the early 20th century. Best remembered for her lyrical, experimental novels, including *Mrs. Dalloway* and *To the Lighthouse*, Woolf also wrote a book-length essay entitled "A Room of One's Own," in which she muses on women as writers and as characters in fiction, describing the many challenges women face in their paths to self-actualization. In this excerpt, Woolf speculates about what might have happened if Shakespeare had had a talented and strong-willed author for a sister. Through this hypothetical scenario, Woolf illustrates the limited opportunities that had historically been available to women.

"She had no chance of learning grammar and logic, let alone of reading Horace and Virgil."

From Chapter Three

1   Let me imagine, since the facts are so hard to come by, what would have happened had Shakespeare had a wonderfully gifted sister, called Judith, let us say. Shakespeare himself went, very probably—his mother was an heiress—to the grammar school, where he may have learnt Latin—Ovid, Virgil and Horace[1]—and the elements of grammar and **logic**. He was, it is well known, a wild boy who **poached** rabbits, perhaps shot a deer, and had, rather sooner than he should have done, to marry a woman in the neighborhood, who bore him a child rather quicker than was right. That escapade sent him to seek his fortune in London. He had, it seemed, a taste for the theatre; he began by holding horses at the stage door. Very soon he got work in the theatre, became a successful actor, and lived at the hub of the universe, meeting everybody, knowing everybody, practicing his art on the boards, exercising his wits in the streets, and even getting access to the palace of the queen. Meanwhile his extraordinarily gifted sister, let us suppose, remained at home. She was as adventurous, as imaginative, as agog to see the world as he was. But she was not sent to school. She had no chance of learning grammar and logic, let alone of reading Horace and Virgil. She picked up a book now and then, one of her brother's perhaps, and read a few pages. But then her parents came in and told her to mend the stockings or mind the stew and not moon about with books and papers. They would have spoken sharply but kindly, for they were **substantial** people who knew the conditions of life for a woman and loved their daughter—indeed, more likely than not she was the apple of her father's eye. Perhaps she scribbled some pages up in an apple loft[2] on the sly, but was careful to hide them or set fire to them. Soon, however, before she was out of her teens, she was to be betrothed to the son of a neighboring wool-stapler. She cried out that marriage was hateful to her, and for that she was severely beaten by her father. Then he ceased to scold her. He begged her instead not to hurt him, not to shame him in this matter of her marriage. He would give her a chain of beads or a fine petticoat, he said; and there were tears in his eyes. How could she disobey him? How could she

1. **Ovid, Virgil, and Horace** three of the most famous poets of ancient Rome
2. **apple loft** an open second storey of a barn

break his heart? The force of her own gift alone drove her to it. She made up a small parcel of her belongings, let herself down by a rope one summer's night and took the road to London. She was not seventeen. The birds that sang in the hedge were not more musical than she was. She had the quickest fancy, a gift like her brother's, for the tune of words. Like him, she had a taste for the theatre. She stood at the stage door; she wanted to act, she said. Men laughed in her face. The manager—a fat, loose-lipped man—guffawed. He bellowed something about poodles dancing and women acting—no woman, he said, could possibly be an actress. He hinted—you can imagine what. She could get no training in her craft. Could she even seek her dinner in a tavern or roam the streets at midnight? Yet her genius was for fiction and lusted to feed abundantly upon the lives of men and women and the study of their ways. At last—for she was very young, oddly like Shakespeare the poet in her face, with the same grey eyes and rounded brows—at last Nick Greene the actor-manager took pity on her; she found herself with child by that gentleman and so—who shall measure the heat and violence of the poet's heart when caught and tangled in a woman's body?—killed herself one winter's night and lies buried at some crossroads where the omnibuses now stop outside the Elephant and Castle[3].

2   That, more or less, is how the story would run, I think, if a woman in Shakespeare's day had had Shakespeare's genius. But for my part, I agree with the deceased bishop[4], if such he was—it is unthinkable that any woman in Shakespeare's day should have had Shakespeare's genius. For genius like Shakespeare's is not born among labouring, uneducated, **servile** people. It was not born in England among the Saxons and the Britons. It is not born today among the working classes. How, then, could it have been born among women whose work began, according to Professor Trevelyan, almost before they were out of the nursery, who were forced to it by their parents and held to it by all the power of law and custom? Yet genius of a sort must have existed among women as it must have existed among the working classes. Now and again an Emily Bronte or a Robert Burns[5] blazes out and proves its presence. But certainly it never got itself on to paper. When, however, one reads of a witch being ducked, of a woman possessed by devils, of a wise woman selling herbs, or even of a very remarkable man who had a mother, then I think we are on the track of a lost novelist, a suppressed poet, of some mute and inglorious Jane Austen, some Emily Bronte who dashed her brains out on the moor or mopped and mowed about the highways crazed with the torture that her gift had put her to. Indeed, I would venture to guess that

---

3. **outside the Elephant and Castle** a road and Underground transportation hub in the Southwark borough of London
4. **the deceased bishop** Virginia Woolf remembers a bishop who wrote that no woman could ever become as smart or accomplished as Shakespeare
5. **Emily Brontë or a Robert Burns** Emily Brontë (1818–1848), author of the classic novel Wuthering Heights; Robert Burns (1759–1796), national poet of Scotland, writer of "Auld Lang Syne"

Anon, who wrote so many poems without signing them, was often a woman. It was a woman Edward Fitzgerald[6], I think, suggested who made the ballads and the folk-songs, crooning them to her children, beguiling her spinning with them, on the length of the winter's night.

3   This may be true or it may be false—who can say?—but what is true in it, so it seemed to me, reviewing the story of Shakespeare's sister as I had made it, is that any woman born with a great gift in the sixteenth century would certainly have gone crazed, shot herself, or ended her days in some lonely cottage outside the village, half witch, half wizard, feared and mocked at. For it needs little skill in psychology to be sure that a highly gifted girl who had tried to use her gift for poetry would have been so thwarted and hindered by other people, so tortured and pulled **asunder** by her own contrary instincts, that she must have lost her health and sanity to a certainty.

Excerpted from *A Room of One's Own* by Virginia Woolf, published by Mariner Books.

✎ WRITE

ARGUMENTATIVE: Woolf states: "Genius like Shakespeare's is not born among labouring, uneducated, servile people." Do you think this statement still holds true today? In an essay response, discuss whether you think "genius" among the "working classes" is possible in today's society, and why or why not. How might this have been different in the time in which Woolf lived, and why?

6. **woman Edward Fitzgerald** Lady Edward FitzGerald (1809–1883), translated quatrains ascribed to the 11th century Persian poet Omar Khayyam that became very popular; later investigations strongly suggested his *Rubáiyát* was largely of FitzGerald's own invention

The New Dress

FICTION
Virginia Woolf
1927

Introduction

English author Virginia Woolf (1882–1941) is widely considered one of the most important literary figures of the 20th century. Woolf was a pioneer in her use of stream-of-consciousness, a narrative technique that follows a character's flow of thoughts. Her short story "The New Dress" was first published in the May 1927 issue of *Forum*, a New York City magazine. Some literary critics suspect that the short story was originally meant as a chapter for *Mrs. Dalloway*, Woolf's best-known novel. Both texts share some of the same characters and were written within three years of one another. In the story, Mabel wears a new handmade yellow dress to one of Mrs. Dalloway's cocktail parties. Deeply self-conscious, Mabel is convinced she is being mocked by the other partygoers.

"What's Mabel wearing? What a fright she looks!"

NOTES

1   Mabel had her first serious suspicion that something was wrong as she took her cloak off and Mrs. Barnet, while handing her the mirror and touching the brushes and thus drawing her attention, perhaps rather markedly, to all the appliances for tidying and improving hair, complexion, clothes, which existed on the dressing table, confirmed

Virginia Woolf

the suspicion—that it was not right, not quite right, which growing stronger as she went upstairs and springing at her, with conviction as she greeted Clarissa Dalloway, she went straight to the far end of the room, to a shaded corner where a looking-glass hung and looked. No! It was not RIGHT. And at once the misery which she always tried to hide, the **profound** dissatisfaction—the sense she had had, ever since she was a child, of being inferior to other people—set upon her, relentlessly, remorselessly, with an intensity which she could not beat off, as she would when she woke at night at home, by reading Borrow or Scott[1]; for oh these men, oh these women, all were thinking— "What's Mabel wearing? What a fright she looks! What a hideous new dress!"— their eyelids flickering as they came up and then their lids shutting rather tight. It was her own appalling inadequacy; her cowardice; her mean, water-sprinkled blood that depressed her. And at once the whole of the room where, for ever so many hours, she had planned with the little dressmaker how it was to go, seemed **sordid**, repulsive; and her own drawing-room so shabby, and herself, going out, puffed up with vanity as she touched the letters on the hall table and said: "How dull!" to show off—all this now seemed unutterably silly, paltry, and provincial. All this had been absolutely destroyed, shown up, exploded, the moment she came into Mrs. Dalloway's drawing-room.

---

1. **Borrow or Scott** George Henry Borrow (1803–1881), travel writer, lived with English gypsies and wrote romantically about their lifestyle; Sir Walter Scott (1771–1832) author of the popular 1819 novel *Ivanhoe*, which presented a romanticized, unrealistic version of England in the Middle Ages

2   What she had thought that evening when, sitting over the teacups, Mrs. Dalloway's invitation came, was that, of course, she could not be fashionable. It was absurd to pretend it even—fashion meant cut, meant style, meant thirty guineas at least—but why not be original? Why not be herself, anyhow? And, getting up, she had taken that old fashion book of her mother's, a Paris fashion book of the time of the Empire, and had thought how much prettier, more dignified, and more womanly they were then, and so set herself—oh, it was foolish—trying to be like them, pluming herself in fact, upon being modest and old-fashioned, and very charming, giving herself up, no doubt about it, to an orgy of self-love, which deserved to be **chastised**, and so rigged herself out like this.

3   But she dared not look in the glass. She could not face the whole horror—the pale yellow, idiotically old-fashioned silk dress with its long skirt and its high sleeves and its waist and all the things that looked so charming in the fashion book, but not on her, not among all these ordinary people. She felt like a dressmaker's dummy standing there, for young people to stick pins into.

4   "But, my dear, it's perfectly charming!" Rose Shaw said, looking her up and down with that little satirical pucker of the lips which she expected—Rose herself being dressed in the height of the fashion, precisely like everybody else, always.

5   We are all like flies trying to crawl over the edge of the saucer, Mabel thought, and repeated the phrase as if she were crossing herself, as if she were trying to find some spell to annul this pain, to make this agony endurable. Tags of Shakespeare, lines from books she had read ages ago, suddenly came to her when she was in agony, and she repeated them over and over again. "Flies trying to crawl," she repeated. If she could say that over often enough and make herself see the flies, she would become numb, chill, frozen, dumb. Now she could see flies crawling slowly out of a saucer of milk with their wings stuck together; and she strained and strained (standing in front of the looking-glass, listening to Rose Shaw) to make herself see Rose Shaw and all the other people there as flies, trying to hoist themselves out of something, or into something, meagre, insignificant, toiling flies. But she could not see them like that, not other people. She saw herself like that—she was a fly, but the others were dragonflies, butterflies, beautiful insects, dancing, fluttering, skimming, while she alone dragged herself up out of the saucer. (Envy and spite, the most detestable of the vices, were her chief faults.)

6   "I feel like some dowdy, decrepit, horribly dingy old fly," she said, making Robert Haydon stop just to hear her say that, just to reassure herself by furbishing up a poor weak-kneed phrase and so showing how detached she was, how witty, that she did not feel in the least out of anything. And, of course, Robert Haydon answered something, quite polite, quite insincere, which she

saw through instantly, and said to herself, directly he went (again from some book), "Lies, lies, lies!" For a party makes things either much more real, or much less real, she thought; she saw in a flash to the bottom of Robert Haydon's heart; she saw through everything. She saw the truth. THIS was true, this drawing-room, this self, and the other false. Miss Milan's little workroom was really terribly hot, stuffy, sordid. It smelt of clothes and cabbage cooking; and yet, when Miss Milan put the glass in her hand, and she looked at herself with the dress on, finished, an extraordinary bliss shot through her heart. Suffused with light, she sprang into existence. Rid of cares and wrinkles, what she had dreamed of herself was there—a beautiful woman. just for a second (she had not dared look longer, Miss Milan wanted to know about the length of the skirt), there looked at her, framed in the scrolloping mahogany, a grey-white, mysteriously smiling, charming girl, the core of herself, the soul of herself; and it was not vanity only, not only self-love that made her think it good, tender, and true. Miss Milan said that the skirt could not well be longer; if anything the skirt, said Miss Milan, puckering her forehead, considering with all her wits about her, must be shorter; and she felt, suddenly, honestly, full of love for Miss Milan, much, much fonder of Miss Milan than of any one in the whole world, and could have cried for pity that she should be crawling on the floor with her mouth full of pins, and her face red and her eyes bulging—that one human being should be doing this for another, and she saw them all as human beings merely, and herself going off to her party, and Miss Milan pulling the cover over the canary's cage, or letting him pick a hemp-seed from between her lips, and the thought of it, of this side of human nature and its patience and its endurance and its being content with such miserable, scanty, sordid, little pleasures filled her eyes with tears.

7   And now the whole thing had vanished. The dress, the room, the love, the pity, the scrolloping looking-glass, and the canary's cage—all had vanished, and here she was in a corner of Mrs. Dalloway's drawing-room, suffering tortures, woken wide awake to reality.

8   But it was all so paltry, weak-blooded, and petty-minded to care so much at her age with two children, to be still so utterly dependent on people's opinions and not have principles or convictions, not to be able to say as other people did, "There's Shakespeare! There's death! We're all weevils in a captain's biscuit"—or whatever it was that people did say.

9   She faced herself straight in the glass; she pecked at her left shoulder; she issued out into the room, as if spears were thrown at her yellow dress from all sides. But instead of looking fierce or tragic, as Rose Shaw would have done—Rose would have looked like Boadicea[2]—she looked foolish and self-

---

2. **Boadicea** tribal queen of the indigenous Celtic Iceni, who led a rebellion against Roman occupation 60–61 CE

conscious, and simpered like a schoolgirl and slouched across the room, positively slinking, as if she were a beaten mongrel, and looked at a picture, an engraving. As if one went to a party to look at a picture! Everybody knew why she did it—it was from shame, from humiliation.

10 "Now the fly's in the saucer," she said to herself, "right in the middle, and can't get out, and the milk," she thought, rigidly staring at the picture, "is sticking its wings together."

11 "It's so old-fashioned," she said to Charles Burt, making him stop (which by itself he hated) on his way to talk to some one else.

12 She meant, or she tried to make herself think that she meant, that it was the picture and not her dress, that was old-fashioned. And one word of praise, one word of affection from Charles would have made all the difference to her at the moment. If he had only said, "Mabel, you're looking charming to-night!" it would have changed her life. But then she ought to have been truthful and direct. Charles said nothing of the kind, of course. He was malice itself. He always saw through one, especially if one were feeling particularly mean, paltry, or feeble-minded.

13 "Mabel's got a new dress!" he said, and the poor fly was absolutely shoved into the middle of the saucer. Really, he would like her to drown, she believed. He had no heart, no fundamental kindness, only a **veneer** of friendliness. Miss Milan was much more real, much kinder. If only one could feel that and stick to it, always. "Why," she asked herself—replying to Charles much too pertly, letting him see that she was out of temper, or "ruffled" as he called it ("Rather ruffled?" he said and went on to laugh at her with some woman over there)—"Why," she asked herself, "can't I feel one thing always, feel quite sure that Miss Milan is right, and Charles wrong and stick to it, feel sure about the canary and pity and love and not be whipped all round in a second by coming into a room full of people?" It was her odious, weak, vacillating character again, always giving at the critical moment and not being seriously interested in conchology, etymology, botany, archeology, cutting up potatoes and watching them fructify like Mary Dennis, like Violet Searle.

14 Then Mrs. Holman, seeing her standing there, bore down upon her. Of course a thing like a dress was beneath Mrs. Holman's notice, with her family always tumbling downstairs or having the scarlet fever. Could Mabel tell her if Elmthorpe was ever let for August and September? Oh, it was a conversation that bored her unutterably!—it made her furious to be treated like a house agent or a messenger boy, to be made use of. Not to have value, that was it, she thought, trying to grasp something hard, something real, while she tried to answer sensibly about the bathroom and the south aspect and the hot water to the top of the house; and all the time she could

Please note that excerpts and passages in the StudySync® library and this workbook are intended as touchstones to generate interest in an author's work. The excerpts and passages do not substitute for the reading of entire texts, and StudySync® strongly recommends that students seek out and purchase the whole literary or informational work in order to experience it as the author intended. Links to online resellers are available in our digital library. In addition, complete works may be ordered through an authorized reseller by filling out and returning to StudySync® the order form enclosed in this workbook.

Reading & Writing Companion 69

see little bits of her yellow dress in the round looking-glass which made them all the size of boot-buttons or tadpoles; and it was amazing to think how much humiliation and agony and self-loathing and effort and passionate ups and downs of feeling were contained in a thing the size of a threepenny bit. And what was still odder, this thing, this Mabel Waring, was separate, quite disconnected; and though Mrs. Holman (the black button) was leaning forward and telling her how her eldest boy had strained his heart running, she could see her, too, quite detached in the looking-glass, and it was impossible that the black dot, leaning forward, gesticulating, should make the yellow dot, sitting solitary, self-centred, feel what the black dot was feeling, yet they pretended.

15   "So impossible to keep boys quiet"—that was the kind of thing one said.

16   And Mrs. Holman, who could never get enough sympathy and snatched what little there was greedily, as if it were her right (but she deserved much more for there was her little girl who had come down this morning with a swollen knee-joint), took this miserable offering and looked at it suspiciously, grudgingly, as if it were a halfpenny when it ought to have been a pound and put it away in her purse, must put up with it, mean and miserly though it was, times being hard, so very hard; and on she went, creaking, injured Mrs. Holman, about the girl with the swollen joints. Ah, it was tragic, this greed, this clamour of human beings, like a row of cormorants, barking and flapping their wings for sympathy—it was tragic, could one have felt it and not merely pretended to feel it!

17   But in her yellow dress to-night she could not wring out one drop more; she wanted it all, all for herself. She knew (she kept on looking into the glass, dipping into that dreadfully showing-up blue pool) that she was condemned, despised, left like this in a backwater, because of her being like this a feeble, vacillating creature; and it seemed to her that the yellow dress was a penance which she had deserved, and if she had been dressed like Rose Shaw, in lovely, clinging green with a ruffle of swansdown, she would have deserved that; and she thought that there was no escape for her—none whatever. But it was not her fault altogether, after all. It was being one of a family of ten; never having money enough, always skimping and paring; and her mother carrying great cans, and the linoleum worn on the stair edges, and one sordid little domestic tragedy after another—nothing catastrophic, the sheep farm failing, but not utterly; her eldest brother marrying beneath him but not very much—there was no romance, nothing extreme about them all. They petered out respectably in seaside resorts; every watering-place had one of her aunts even now asleep in some lodging with the front windows not quite facing the sea. That was so like them—they had to squint at things always. And she had done the same—she was just like her aunts. For all her dreams of living in India, married to some hero like Sir Henry

Lawrence[3], some empire builder (still the sight of a native in a turban filled her with romance), she had failed utterly. She had married Hubert, with his safe, permanent underling's job in the Law Courts, and they managed tolerably in a smallish house, without proper maids, and hash when she was alone or just bread and butter, but now and then—Mrs. Holman was off, thinking her the most dried-up, unsympathetic twig she had ever met, absurdly dressed, too, and would tell every one about Mabel's fantastic appearance—now and then, thought Mabel Waring, left alone on the blue sofa, punching the cushion in order to look occupied, for she would not join Charles Burt and Rose Shaw, chattering like magpies and perhaps laughing at her by the fireplace—now and then, there did come to her delicious moments, reading the other night in bed, for instance, or down by the sea on the sand In the sun, at Easter—let her recall it—a great tuft of pale sand-grass standing all twisted like a shock of spears against the sky, which was blue like a smooth china egg[4], so firm, so hard, and then the melody of the waves—"Hush, hush," they said, and the children's shouts paddling—yes, it was a divine moment, and there she lay, she felt, in the hand of the Goddess who was the world; rather a hard-hearted, but very beautiful Goddess, a little lamb laid on the altar (one did think these silly things, and it didn't matter so long as one never said them). And also with Hubert sometimes she had quite unexpectedly—carving the mutton for Sunday lunch, for no reason, opening a letter, coming into a room—divine moments, when she said to herself (for she would never say this to anybody else), "This is it. This has happened. This is it!" And the other way about it was equally surprising—that is, when everything was arranged—music, weather, holidays, every reason for happiness was there—then nothing happened at all. One wasn't happy. It was flat, just flat, that was all.

18   Her wretched self again, no doubt! She had always been a fretful, weak, unsatisfactory mother, a wobbly wife, lolling about in a kind of twilight existence with nothing very clear or very bold, or more one thing than another, like all her brothers and sisters, except perhaps Herbert—they were all the same poor water-veined creatures who did nothing. Then in the midst of this creeping, crawling life, suddenly she was on the crest of a wave. That wretched fly—where had she read the story that kept coming into her mind about the fly and the saucer?—struggled out. Yes, she had those moments. But now that she was forty, they might come more and more seldom. By degrees she would cease to struggle any more. But that was deplorable! That was not to be **endured**! That made her feel ashamed of herself!

---

3. **Sir Henry Lawrence** Brigadier General Sir Henry Montgomery Lawrence (1806–1857), a British colonial administrator in India who was killed at the Siege of Lucknow
4. **china egg** a decorative egg made of porcelain

19 She would go to the London Library to-morrow. She would find some wonderful, helpful, astonishing book, quite by chance, a book by a clergyman, by an American no one had ever heard of; or she would walk down the Strand and drop, accidentally, into a hall where a miner was telling about the life in the pit, and suddenly she would become a new person. She would be absolutely transformed. She would wear a uniform; she would be called Sister Somebody; she would never give a thought to clothes again. And for ever after she would be perfectly clear about Charles Burt and Miss Milan and this room and that room; and it would be always, day after day, as if she were lying in the sun or carving the mutton. It would be it!

20 So she got up from the blue sofa, and the yellow button in the looking-glass got up too, and she waved her hand to Charles and Rose to show them she did not depend on them one scrap, and the yellow button moved out of the looking-glass, and all the spears were gathered into her breast as she walked towards Mrs. Dalloway and said "Good night."

21 "But it's too early to go," said Mrs. Dalloway, who was always so charming.

22 "I'm afraid I must," said Mabel Waring. "But," she added in her weak, wobbly voice which only sounded ridiculous when she tried to strengthen it, "I have enjoyed myself enormously."

23 'I have enjoyed myself," she said to Mr. Dalloway, whom she met on the stairs.

24 "Lies, lies, lies!" she said to herself, going downstairs, and "Right in the saucer!" she said to herself as she thanked Mrs. Barnet for helping her and wrapped herself, round and round and round, in the Chinese cloak she had worn these twenty years.

✏ WRITE

NARRATIVE: Compose a brief passage of a short story focusing on a character whose outward appearance does not match his or her feelings. Use "The New Dress" as a model, because the main character in the story secretly thinks she looks hideous while she tries to put a brave face on her situation. Consider how it might affect a person to hide his or her true feelings at a party or with a single person who is important to him or her.

Hurricane Season

POETRY
Fareena Arefeen
2016

Introduction

In September of 2008, Hurricane Ike roared through Haiti and Cuba, traveled up the Gulf of Mexico, and barreled into Texas with increasing velocity, causing broken windows, flooded streets and numerous casualties. Houston-area poet Fareena Arefeen channels her own memories of the city's natural disasters in "Hurricane Season," an energetic meditation on her connection to Houston as a first-generation immigrant and her desire to wield language to create art. While a junior at Houston's High School for Performing and Visual Arts, Arefeen was named the city's second Youth Poet Laureate in 2016.

"I only came into my skin after I grew into this city"

1. My mother tells me that I was born outside of the eye of a hurricane,
2. where the storm is strong and moves quickly in **radials**.
3. I think I am a series of low pressure systems and winds that can carry **bayous**.

4. I've heard that a child playing on the coast in Africa
5. can cause the start of a hurricane in the Atlantic and maybe
6. a working immigrant in Toronto can be the origin of a poet in Houston.

7. My ninth birthday was suspended in the space between **cyclone** and serene.
8. I watched my city build itself up again after Hurricane Ike and
9. I guess we are both having growing pains.

10. I've learned that my purpose is flooding.
11. I want to form inundacions of words and earn
12. the title of a Category Four[1]. Drought relief and filler of bayou banks.
13. Hurricanes bring heat energy from the tropics
14. the way I would like to bring light to the city that taught me how to hold rainwater in the form of letters.

15. On my thirteenth birthday, I watched the bayou
16. spill into this dizzy headed space city
17. like a push of blood to the lungs.

18. Inhaling **atmospheric** pressure of a tropical storm
19. in the eye of hurricane season felt like bayou backwash
20. of building Rothko[2] layers.

21. Maybe if I could say that brown is my favorite color,
22. I would finally see the whirlpools that rest in my skin and in the Buffalo Bayou.
23. And someday I could love the greens hidden in browns hidden in **labyrinths** of color.

---

1. **Category Four** hurricanes or cyclones are measured for force on a five-level scale, five being the most powerful
2. **Rothko** Mark Rothko (1903–1970), abstract expressionist painter and creator of Houston's Rothko Chapel

24 I only came into my skin
25 after I grew into this city and they both happened like storm clouds; rolling in
and all at once.

26 Now, I find impressions of myself in the silt
27 as there are maps of this city pressed into my hands like footsteps on wet
ground.

28 On my seventeenth birthday, the clouds broke light rays
29 the way I want to leave fractures in my city
30 that can be filled with the work of new artists and immigrants to take my
place.

31 My favorite smell is rain
32 falling through concrete and cumin³ because they combine homes.
33 I can be a drop of water falling in multiple places.

34 I am stuck to the city I've learned to call my own
35 like humidity on skin that can finally
36 hold its own storm.

By Fareena Arefeen, 2016. Used by permission of Fareena Arefeen.

✏ WRITE

LITERARY ANALYSIS: Arefeen uses the image of a hurricane to express a wide variety of personal experiences; at times the speaker seems to be the hurricane itself, while at other times the speaker seems to be in the midst of experiencing a hurricane. Is the image of a hurricane in this poem creative, destructive, or both? Cite textual evidence to support your argument.

---

3. **cumin** a powdery spice derived from the crushed seeds of a flowering plant, commonly used in Bengali cuisine

Be Ye Men of Valour

ARGUMENTATIVE TEXT
Winston Churchill
1940

Introduction

Delivered on May 19, 1940, "Be Ye Men of Valour" was Winston Churchill's (1874–1965) first radio address as British Prime Minister. In the speech, Churchill acknowledges that German military aggression would likely soon be directed at Great Britain, and tells his countrymen not to be intimidated. Instead, he urges them to prepare to do whatever is necessary to defeat a formidable adversary.

"Our task is not only to win the battle—but to win the war."

1   I speak to you for the first time as Prime Minister in a solemn hour for the life of our country, of our empire, of our allies, and, above all, of the cause of freedom. A tremendous battle is raging in France and Flanders[1]. The Germans, by a remarkable combination of air bombing and heavily armored tanks, have broken through the French defenses north of the Maginot Line[2], and strong columns of their armored vehicles are ravaging the open country, which for the first day or two was without defenders. They have penetrated deeply and spread alarm and confusion in their track. Behind them there are now appearing infantry in lorries[3], and behind them, again, the large **masses** are moving forward. The re-groupment of the French armies to make head against, and also to strike at, this intruding wedge has been proceeding for several days, largely assisted by the magnificent efforts of the Royal Air Force.

British prime minister Winston Churchill (1874–1965) inspects bomb damage outside the London offices of the British Equitable Assurance after a World War II air raid, 10th September 1940.

Skill:
Central or
Main Idea

While there is a lot of other information here, the main idea of this first paragraph is that war is raging and Britain (Churchill's audience) is in great danger. The additional details describe what is happening with the war.

2   We must not allow ourselves to be intimidated by the presence of these armored vehicles in unexpected places behind our lines. If they are behind our Front, the French are also at many points fighting actively behind theirs. Both sides are therefore in an extremely dangerous position. And if the French Army and our own Army are well handled, as I believe they will be, if the French retain that genius for recovery and counter-attack for which they have so long been famous, and if the British Army shows the dogged endurance and solid fighting power of which there have been so many examples in the past, then a sudden transformation of the scene might spring into being.

---

1. **Flanders** the northern area of Belgium, encompassing Brussels
2. **the Maginot Line** a line of fortifications built in the 1930s along the French border to prevent German invasion
3. **lorry** (British) truck

NOTES

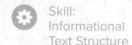

Skill:
Word Meaning

What does grapples
mean? It appears to be
an action taken "with
the enemy" by a man,
an officer, a brigade,
or a division, so I'm
guessing it's a verb. It
also looks a bit like
"grape," but I'm not
sure about that
connection.

Skill:
Informational
Text Structure

Early in his speech,
Churchill appeals to
pathos, presenting
images of "ruin and
slavery . . . turned upon
us." With listeners in an
emotional state, he
unfolds his thesis:
Britain is ready to fight
and will do everything
to win.

3   Now it would be foolish, however, to disguise the gravity of the hour. It would be still more foolish to lose heart and courage or to suppose that well-trained, well-equipped armies numbering three or four millions of men can be overcome in the space of a few weeks, or even months, by a scoop, or raid of mechanized vehicles, however **formidable**. We may look with confidence to the stabilization of the Front in France, and to the general engagement of the masses, which will enable the qualities of the French and British soldiers to be matched squarely against those of their adversaries. For myself, I have invincible confidence in the French Army and its leaders. Only a very small part of that splendid Army has yet been heavily engaged; and only a very small part of France has yet been invaded. There is a good evidence to show that practically the whole of the specialized and mechanized forces of the enemy have been already thrown into the battle; and we know that very heavy losses have been inflicted upon them. No officer or man, no brigade or division, which grapples at close quarters with the enemy, wherever encountered, can fail to make a worthy contribution to the general result. The Armies must cast away the idea of resisting attack behind concrete lines or natural obstacles, and must realize that mastery can only be regained by furious and unrelenting assault. And this spirit must not only animate the High Command, but must inspire every fighting man.

4   In the air—often at serious odds, often at odds hitherto thought overwhelming— we have been clawing down three or four to one of our enemies; and the relative balance of the British and German Air Forces is now considerably more favorable to us than at the beginning of the battle. In cutting down the German bombers, we are fighting our own battle as well as that of France. My confidence in our ability to fight it out to the finish with the German Air Force has been strengthened by the fierce encounters which have taken place and are taking place. At the same time, our heavy bombers are striking nightly at the tap-root of German mechanized power, and have already inflicted serious damage upon the oil refineries on which the Nazi effort to dominate the world directly depends.

5   We must expect that as soon as stability is reached on the Western Front, the bulk of that hideous apparatus of aggression which gashed Holland into ruin and slavery in a few days will be turned upon us. I am sure I speak for all when I say we are ready to face it, to endure it, and to retaliate against it to any extent that the unwritten laws of war permit. There will be many men and many women in this Island who, when the ordeal comes upon them, as come it will, will feel comfort, and even a pride, that they are sharing the perils of our lads at the Front—soldiers, sailors, and airmen—God bless them—and are drawing away from them a part at least of the onslaught they have to bear. Is not this the appointed time for all to make the utmost exertions in their power? If the battle is to be won, we must provide our men with ever-increasing quantities of the weapons and ammunition they need. We must have, and have quickly, more aeroplanes, more tanks, more shells, more guns. There is imperious need for

these vital munitions. They increase our strength against the powerfully armed enemy. They replace the wastage of the obstinate struggle—and the knowledge that wastage will speedily be replaced enables us to draw more readily upon our reserves and throw them in now that everything counts so much.

6   Our task is not only to win the battle—but to win the war. After this battle in France **abates** its force, there will come the battle for our Island—for all Britain is, and all that Britain means. That will be the struggle. In that supreme emergency we shall not hesitate to take every step, even the most drastic, to call forth from our people the last ounce and the last inch of effort of which they are capable. The interests of property, the hours of labor, are nothing compared to the struggle for life and honor, for right and freedom, to which we have vowed ourselves.

7   I have received from the Chiefs of the French Republic, and in particular from its indomitable Prime Minister, Monsieur Reynaud, the most sacred pledges that whatever happens they will fight to the end, be it bitter or be it glorious. Nay, if we fight to the end, it can only be glorious.

8   Having received His Majesty's **commission**, I have formed an Administration of men and women of every Party and of almost every point of view. We have differed and quarreled in the past, but now one bond unites us all: to wage war until victory is won, and never to surrender ourselves to servitude and shame, whatever the cost and the agony may be. This is one of the most awe-striking periods in the long history of France and Britain. It is also beyond doubt the most sublime. Side by side, unaided except by their kith and kin in the great Dominions[4] and by the wide empires which rest beneath their shield—side by side the British and French peoples have advanced to rescue not only Europe but mankind from the foulest and most soul-destroying tyranny which has ever darkened and stained the pages of history. Behind them, behind us, behind the Armies and Fleets of Britain and France, gather a group of shattered States and bludgeoned races: the Czechs, the Poles, the Norwegians, the Danes, the Dutch, the Belgians—upon all of whom the long night of barbarism will descend, unbroken even by a star of hope, unless we conquer, as conquer we must, as conquer we shall.

9   Today is Trinity Sunday[5]. Centuries ago words were written to be a call and a spur to the faithful servants of truth and justice:

10 Arm yourselves, and be ye men of **valour**, and be in readiness for the conflict; for it is better for us to perish in battle than to look upon the outrage of our nation and our altars. As the will of God is in Heaven, even so let it be.

---

4. **the great Dominions** referring to the colonized lands of the British Empire in Africa, India, Southeast Asia, the Pacific and the Caribbean
5. **Trinity Sunday** the eighth Sunday after Easter in the Christian liturgical calendar, celebrating the Trinity of God, Jesus, and the Holy Spirit

Skill:
Informational
Text Structure

Churchill continues his appeal to pathos here, saying "all Britain" could be lost. He then reasserts his position that Britain needs to "take every step" and that Britons will need to accept "even the most drastic" efforts.

Skill:
Central or
Main Idea

All the way through to the conclusion, the main ideas from the beginning are supported: Although the situation is legitimately dangerous, there is hope. But only if Britain acts with bravery and determination.

First Read

Read "Be Ye Men of Valour." After you read, complete the Think Questions below.

 THINK QUESTIONS

1. What is the current state of the war, and why does Churchill feel such a sense of urgency? Use details from the text to support your inferences.

2. How is what Churchill says about France in paragraph 1 different from what he says in paragraph 3? What reaction do you infer he hopes to elicit from his audience by making these two conflicting points? Support your inferences with evidence from the text.

3. Who are the "group of shattered States and bludgeoned races"? What image of Britain and France does Churchill hope to convey with this reference? Support your answer with evidence from the text.

4. Use context clues to find the definition of **formidable** as it is used in the text. Write your definition here, and explain which clues helped you arrive at it.

5. Write your definition for the word **commission** as it appears in the text. Then use a print or online dictionary to confirm the definition.

Skill:
Informational Text Structure

Use the Checklist to analyze Informational Text Structure in "Be Ye Men of Valour." Refer to the sample student annotations about Informational Text Structure in the text.

••• CHECKLIST FOR INFORMATIONAL TEXT STRUCTURE

In order to determine the structure an author uses in his or her exposition or argument, note the following:

- ✓ where the author introduces and clarifies their argument

- ✓ sentences and paragraphs that reveal the text structure the author uses to frame the argument

- ✓ whether the text structure is effective in presenting all sides of the argument, and makes his or her points clear, convincing and engaging

To analyze and evaluate the effectiveness of the structure an author uses in his or her exposition or argument, including whether the structure makes points clear, convincing, and engaging, consider the following questions:

- ✓ Did I have to read a particular sentence or phrase over again? Where?

- ✓ Did I find myself distracted or uninterested while reading the text? When?

- ✓ Did the structure the author used make their points clear, convincing, and engaging? Why or why not?

- ✓ Was the author's exposition or argument effective? Why or why not?

Please note that excerpts and passages in the StudySync® library and this workbook are intended as touchstones to generate interest in an author's work. The excerpts and passages do not substitute for the reading of entire texts, and StudySync® strongly recommends that students seek out and purchase the whole literary or informational work in order to experience it as the author intended. Links to online resellers are available in our digital library. In addition, complete works may be ordered through an authorized reseller by filling out and returning to StudySync® the order form enclosed in this workbook.

Reading & Writing
Companion

81

Skill:
Informational Text Structure

Reread paragraph 8 of "Be Ye Men of Valour." Then, using the Checklist on the previous page, answer the multiple-choice questions below.

⟳ YOUR TURN

1. This question has two parts. First, answer Part A. Then, answer Part B.

   Part A: The central argument of this excerpt can best be described as—

   ○ A. "The Danes have been soundly defeated by the Nazis."

   ○ B. "Britain and France both have very large empires."

   ○ C. "Britain and France must and will defeat the Nazis."

   ○ D. "To defeat the Nazis, Britain and France must act as tyrants."

   Part B: Which of the following sentences or phrases from the text best supports your answer to Part A.

   ○ A. "This is one of the most awe-striking periods in the long history of France and Britain."

   ○ B. "Behind them, behind us, behind the Armies and Fleets of Britain and France, gather a group of shattered States and bludgeoned races."

   ○ C. "upon all of whom the long night of barbarism will descend, unbroken even by a star of hope"

   ○ D. "as conquer we must, as conquer we shall"

2. In using the phrase "foulest and most soul-destroying tyranny," Churchill is most clearly—

   ○ A. making an appeal to his audience's reason.

   ○ B. making an appeal to his audience's emotions.

   ○ C. explaining that Britain has no chance of winning the war.

   ○ D. explaining that Britain and France are very close friends.

Skill:
Central or Main Idea

Use the Checklist to analyze Central or Main Idea in "Be Ye Men of Valour." Refer to the sample student annotations about Central or Main Idea in the text.

••• CHECKLIST FOR CENTRAL OR MAIN IDEA

In order to identify two or more central ideas of a text, note the following:

✓ the main idea in each paragraph or group of paragraphs

✓ key details in each paragraph or section of text, distinguishing what they have in common

✓ whether the details contain information that could indicate more than one main idea in a text

• a science text, for example, may provide information about a specific environment and also a message on ecological awareness

• a biography may contain equally important ideas about a person's achievements, influence, and the time period in which the person lives or lived

✓ when each central idea emerges

✓ ways that the central ideas interact and build on one another

To determine two or more central ideas of a text and analyze their development over the course of the text, including how they interact and build on one another to provide a complex analysis, consider the following questions:

✓ What main idea(s) do the details in each paragraph explain or describe?

✓ What central or main ideas do all the paragraphs support?

✓ How do the central ideas interact and build on one another? How does that affect when they emerge?

✓ How might you provide an objective summary of the text? What details would you include?

Skill:
Central or Main Idea

Reread paragraph 8 of "Be Ye Men of Valour." Then, using the Checklist on the previous page, answer the multiple-choice questions below.

⟳ YOUR TURN

1. This question has two parts. First, answer Part A. Then, answer Part B.

   Part A: Which of the following is the best restatement of the central idea of this paragraph?

   ○ A. Regardless of the cost, Britain will sacrifice everything to protect the rest of Europe from Nazi domination.

   ○ B. Regardless of the cost, France and Britain together must save humankind from the evils of Nazi domination.

   ○ C. Although Britain has had some internal strife, it is time to put all that aside and bond together to fight Nazi Germany.

   ○ D. Although it is unlikely that France and Germany will defeat Nazi Germany, they must try for the good of humankind.

   Part B: Which content from the paragraph best supports the answer to Part A?

   ○ A. "Having received His Majesty's commission, I have formed an Administration of men and women of every Party and of almost every point of view."

   ○ B. "We have differed and quarreled in the past, but now one bond unites us all . . ."

   ○ C. "This is one of the most awe-striking periods in the long history of France and Britain."

   ○ D. ". . . side by side the British and French peoples have advanced to rescue not only Europe but mankind from the foulest and most soul-destroying tyranny . . ."

Skill:
Word Meaning

Use the Checklist to analyze Word Meaning in "Be Ye Men of Valour." Refer to the sample student annotations about Word Meaning in the text.

••• CHECKLIST FOR WORD MEANING

In order to find the pronunciation of a word or determine or clarify its precise meaning, do the following:

- ✓ determine the word's part of speech

- ✓ use context clues to make an inferred meaning of the word or phrase

- ✓ consult a dictionary to verify your preliminary determination of the meaning of a word or phrase

- ✓ be sure to read all of the definitions, and then decide which definition makes sense within the context of the text

In order to determine or clarify a word's part of speech, do the following:

- ✓ determine what the word is describing

- ✓ identify how the word is being used in the phrase or sentence

In order to determine the etymology of a word, or its origin or standard usage, do the following:

- ✓ use reference materials, such as a dictionary, to determine the word's origin and history

- ✓ consider how the historical context of the word clarifies its usage

To determine or clarify the etymology or standard usage of a word, consider the following questions:

- ✓ How formal or informal is this word?

- ✓ What is the word describing? What inferred meanings can I make?

- ✓ In what context is the word being used?

- ✓ Is this slang? An example of vernacular? In what other contexts might this word be used?

- ✓ What is the etymology of this word?

Skill:
Word Meaning

Reread the first sentence of paragraph 4 of "Be Ye Men of Valour." Then, using the Checklist on the previous page, answer the multiple-choice questions below.

⟳ YOUR TURN

1. What part of speech is the word *favorable*? How do you know?

   ○ A. It is a verb because it describes how the British Air Force is "clawing down" three or four Germans plans for every one British plan that the Germans are shooting down.

   ○ B. It is an adverb because it describes how the British Air Force is "clawing down" three or four Germans plans for every one British plan that the Germans are shooting down.

   ○ C. It is an adjective because it describes the relative balance of the British and German Air Forces at the time of the speech compared with at the beginning of the battle.

   ○ D. It is a noun because it describes the relative balance of the British and German Air Forces at the time of the speech compared with at the beginning of the battle.

2. Which of the following definitions of *favorable* is most accurate for this context?

   ○ A. expressing approval or support

   ○ B. giving consent; allowing something to happen

   ○ C. giving advantage to someone or something

   ○ D. suggesting a good outcome

Close Read

Reread "Be Ye Men of Valour." As you reread, complete the Skills Focus questions below. Then use your answers and annotations from the questions to help you complete the Write activity.

◎ SKILLS FOCUS

1. Highlight the first sentence of Churchill's speech. What is the most likely meaning of *solemn* in this context? What part of speech is this word, and how do you know? Refer to a dictionary. What is the best definition of this word, given its usage in this passage?

2. Highlight a call to action Churchill makes to his listeners, and explain why it is an effective text structure to help him achieve his purpose.

3. Identify a passage that gives details about events in Europe. Explain how these details support the main idea of Churchill's speech.

4. Identify a passage that reveals Churchill's main idea, and explain how his word choice effectively communicates that idea to his audience.

5. Churchill's speech takes place during one of the most important turning points in modern history. Highlight two examples of Churchill discussing division and alienation, and two examples of Churchill discussing bonding and collaboration. What were the causes of the division? Why is coming together so important at this time?

✏ WRITE

RHETORICAL ANALYSIS: Informational text structure can be used skillfully to compose ideas in a way that heightens the persuasive power of a speech or written work. Write a response in which you summarize the main argument of Churchill's speech and evaluate the structure of the speech. In your response, address the following question: Does the arrangement of ideas make the speech more persuasive? Remember to support your response with textual evidence.

The Pearl Divers' Daughters

POETRY
Marci Calabretta Cancio-Bello
2016

Introduction

Marci Calabretta Cancio-Bello (b. 1989) was a John S. and James L. Knight Fellow at Florida International University before the publication of her first book, *Hour of the Ox*, which won the 2015 Donald Hall Prize for Poetry. She is a teacher and editor, and her poetry has been featured in dozens of journals and anthologies, including *Best New Poets 2015*, a collection featuring 50 up-and-coming young poets. "The Pearl Divers' Daughters" explores the lives and legacy of haenyeo, the legendary female divers of South Korea's Jeju province.

"... pearl divers whose songs build and blossom like barrel-fires or anemones."

NOTES

1 We are the pearl divers' daughters
2 skinning the ocean of her abalone[1] scales,
3 planting oyster seeds in each other's vertebrae.

4 Our mothers carved veins into the sea
5 with **reinvented** air, wrists scarred in rows and rings—
6 octopi and coral—legs scissoring against the sun,

7 the space between their thighs **profound** as trenches.
8 Haenyeo, we name them, pearl divers whose songs build
9 and blossom like barrel-fires or anemones[2].

10 They press our shoulders against the ribs
11 of whale sharks, our palms on dotted black rays.
12 We graze our fingers through damselfish[3] schools,

13 but our appetites are as **insatiate** as the sea is for land.
14 We gnaw the shore, legs wound in seaweed,
15 skin flayed by the tongues of clams, pulling, pushing.

16 Arirang[4], our mothers say patriotically, and cities
17 bloom from our spines, rooting us to **cartographies**,
18 thumbing our eyes into sand-locked jewels.

---

1. **abalone** a general name for sea snails, eaten cooked and raw all over the world
2. **anemones** sea invertebrates resembling the flowering plant for which they are named; they are sedentary or slow-moving and capture fish and marine animals for food
3. **damselfish** brightly hued fish of the family Pomacentridae, often characterized by two contrasting colors that meet horizontally along the middle of the body
4. **Arirang** traditional Korean folk song about a tragic romance that is the national anthem of both North and South Korea

19 We are the pearl divers' daughters,
20 our sisters' skirts are **hemmed** in coral,
21 our brothers are cloud-eyed eels.

22 Arirang, we say, our futures pearled
23 into every empty shell, our tongues pressed
24 against the words until we become them.

A group of 'Haenyeo' on South Korea's southern island of Jeju. Haenyeo, or 'sea women', refers to women who use free-diving to retrieve shell fish from the sea floor.

"The Pearl Divers' Daughters" from *Hour of the Ox*, by Marci Calabretta Cancio-Bello, © 2016. All rights are controlled by the University of Pittsburgh Press, Pittsburgh, PA 15260. Used by permission of the University of Pittsburgh Press.

✎ WRITE

EXPLANATORY: Marci Calabretta Cancio-Bello weaves references to pearl diving in the Korean province of Jeju throughout her poem "The Pearl Divers' Daughters." Analyze the images she presents to determine the actions and tasks that these pearl divers undertake as part of their job. Then, conduct informal research about pearl diving in another particular culture or time period. How do the methods and customs of pearl diving described in "The Pearl Divers' Daughters" align with or depart from those of the culture or time period you researched? Remember to use textual evidence and your research to support your response.

Killers Of The Dream

INFORMATIONAL TEXT
Lillian Smith
1949

Introduction

Lillian Smith (1897–1966) wrote *Killers Of The Dream*, her 1949 memoir, to challenge Southern taboos and unpack the moral and psychological costs of segregation. Written before the American civil rights movement of the 1950s and 60s, her critique of social mores about race and sin influenced those who would later stand up for racial equality. In this excerpt from the first chapter of her book, she reveals that she learned to discriminate as a child, and that these destructive lessons about maintaining white privilege were taught to her by people she loved and trusted—her own parents.

"This haunted childhood belongs to every southerner of my age."

1   Even its children knew that the South was in trouble. No one had to tell them; no words said aloud. To them, it was a vague thing weaving in and out of their play, like a ghost haunting an old graveyard or whispers after the household sleeps—fleeting mystery, vague menace to which each responded in his own way. Some learned to screen out all except the soft and the soothing; others denied even as they saw plainly, and heard. But all knew that under quiet words and warmth and laughter, under the slow ease and tender concern about small matters, there was a heavy burden on all of us and as heavy a refusal to confess it. The children knew this "trouble" was bigger than they, bigger than their family, bigger than their church, so big that people turned away from its size. They had seen it flash out and shatter a town's peace, had felt it tear up all they believed in. They had measured its giant strength and felt weak when they remembered.

2   This haunted childhood belongs to every southerner of my age. We ran away from it but we came back like a hurt animal to its wound, or a murderer to the scene of his sin. The human heart dares not stay away too long from that which hurt it most. There is a return journey to anguish that few of us are released from making.

3   We who were born in the South called this mesh of feeling and memory "loyalty." We thought of it sometimes as "love." We identified with the South's trouble as if we, individually, were responsible for all of it. We defended the sins and the sorrow of three hundred years as if each sin had been committed by us alone and each sorrow had cut across our heart. We were as hurt at criticism of our region as if our own name had been called aloud by the critic. We knew guilt without understanding it, and there is no tie that binds men closer to the past and each other than that.

4   It is a strange thing, this umbilical cord uncut. In times of ease, we do not feel its pull, but when we are threatened with change, suddenly it draws the wholewhite South together in a collective fear and fury that wipe our minds clear of reason and we are blocked from sensible contact with the world we live in.

5   To keep this resistance strong, wall after wall was thrown up in the southern mind against criticism from without and within. Imaginations closed tight against the hurt of others; a regional armoring that took place to ward off the "enemies" who would make our trouble different—or maybe rid us of it completely. For it was a trouble that we did not want to give up. We were as involved with it as a child who cannot be happy at home and cannot bear to tear himself away, or as a grownup who has fallen in love with his own disease. We southerners had identified with the long sorrowful past on such deep levels of love and hate and guilt that we did not know how to break old bonds without pulling our lives down. *Change* was the evil word, a shrill clanking that made us know too well our servitude. *Change* meant leaving one's memories, one's sins, one's **ambivalent** pleasures, the room where one was born.

6   In this South I lived as a child and now live. And it is of it that my story is made. I shall not tell, here, of experiences that were different and special and belonged only to me, but those most white southerners born at the turn of the century share with each other. Out of the intricate weaving of unnumbered threads, I shall pick out a few strands, a few designs that have to do with what we call color and race . . . and politics . . . and money and how it is made . . . and religion . . . and sex and the body image . . . and love . . . and dreams of the Good and the killers of dreams.

7   A southern child's basic lessons were woven of such **dissonant** strands as these; sometimes the threads tangled into a terrifying mess; sometimes **archaic**, startling designs would appear in the weaving; sometimes a design was left broken while another was completed with minute care. Bewildered teachers, bewildered pupils in home and on the street, driven by an invisible Authority, learned their lessons:

8   The mother who taught me what I know of tenderness and love and compassion taught me also the bleak rituals of keeping Negroes in their "place." The father who rebuked me for an air of superiority toward schoolmates from the mill and rounded out his rebuke by gravely reminding me that "all men are brothers," trained me in the steel-rigid **decorums** I must demand of every colored male. They who so gravely taught me to split my body from my mind and both from my "soul," taught me also to split my conscience from my acts and Christianity from southern tradition.

9   Neither the Negro nor sex was often discussed at length in our home. We were given no formal instruction in these difficult matters but we learned our lessons well. We learned the intricate system of taboos, of **renunciations** and compensations, of manners, voice modulations, words, feelings, along with our prayers, our toilet habits, and our games. I do not remember how or when, but by the time I had learned that God is love, that Jesus is His Son and came to give us more abundant life, that all men are brothers with a common

NOTES

Father, I also knew that I was better than a Negro, that all black folks have their place and must be kept in it, that sex has its place and must be kept in it, that a terrifying disaster would befall the South if I ever treated a Negro as my social equal and as terrifying a disaster would befall my family if ever I were to have a baby outside of marriage. I had learned that God so loved the world that He gave His only begotten Son so that we might have segregated churches in which it was my duty to worship each Sunday and on Wednesday at evening prayers. I had learned that white southerners are a hospitable, courteous, tactful people who treat those of their own group with consideration and who as carefully segregate from all the richness of life "for their own good and welfare" thirteen million people whose skin is colored a little differently from my own.

Excerpted from *Killers Of The Dream* by Lillian Smith, published by W.W. Norton & Company.

✏ WRITE

PERSONAL RESPONSE: Near the beginning of the passage, Smith says "The human heart dares not stay away too long from that which hurt it most." Do you agree with this claim? Do you think people are somehow drawn back to places, events, or circumstances that have hurt them in the past? Present your response to this idea using textual evidence as well as experiences of people you have researched or learned about.

Shooting an Elephant

INFORMATIONAL TEXT
George Orwell
1936

Introduction

A British novelist, essayist and social commentator, George Orwell (1903–1950) often wrote about the complex and sometimes destructive relationship between a nation's government and its citizens. One of Orwell's most famous and influential works is *1984*, a dystopian novel set in a future where a totalitarian regime exerts almost complete control over the actions, feelings, and thoughts of its citizens. While touching on similar themes and political undertones, "Shooting an Elephant" is a short, autobiographical piece depicting Orwell's experiences living and working in Burma (known commonly today as Myanmar) in the early 1920s. These experiences would forever inform Orwell's views on imperialism, totalitarianism, and what it means to be truly free.

"In a job like that you see the dirty work of Empire at close quarters."

NOTES

1   In Moulmein, in Lower Burma[1], I was hated by large numbers of people—the only time in my life that I have been important enough for this to happen to me. I was sub-divisional police officer of the town, and in an aimless, petty kind of way anti-European feeling was very bitter. No one had the guts to raise a riot, but if a European woman went through the bazaars[2] alone somebody would probably spit betel juice[3] over her dress. As a police officer I was an obvious target and was baited whenever it seemed safe to do so. When a nimble Burman tripped me up on the football field and the referee (another Burman) looked the other way, the crowd yelled with hideous laughter. This happened more than once. In the end the sneering yellow faces of young men that met me everywhere, the insults hooted after me when I was at a safe distance, got badly on my nerves. The young Buddhist[4] priests were the worst of all. There were several thousands of them in the town and none of them seemed to have anything to do except stand on street corners and jeer at Europeans.

Changing quarters in Upper Burma: baggage elephants arriving in camp, engraving by Paul Naumann from The Illustrated London News, No 2585, November 3, 1888.

2   All this was perplexing and upsetting. For at that time I had already made up my mind that imperialism was an evil thing and the sooner I chucked up my job and got out of it the better. Theoretically—and secretly, of course—I was all for the Burmese and all against their **oppressors**, the British. As for the job

1. **Lower Burma** the coastal area of Myanmar, formerly Burma, incorporated into the British Empire in 1852
2. **bazaar** open public market where small producers, growers, and craftspeople sell their wares
3. **betel juice** the resulting liquid that is regularly spit out in the popular Southeast Asian habit of chewing betel leaves
4. **Buddhist** a follower of Buddhism, a variety of spiritual practices based on teachings of Gautama Buddha, an Indian monk who lived between the 6th and 4th centuries BCE

I was doing, I hated it more bitterly than I can perhaps make clear. In a job like that you see the dirty work of Empire at close quarters. The wretched prisoners huddling in the stinking cages of the lock-ups, the grey, cowed faces of the long-term convicts, the scarred buttocks of the men who had been flogged with bamboos—all these oppressed me with an intolerable sense of guilt. But I could get nothing into perspective. I was young and ill-educated and I had had to think out my problems in the utter silence that is imposed on every Englishman in the East. I did not even know that the British Empire is dying, still less did I know that it is a great deal better than the younger empires that are going to supplant it. All I knew was that I was stuck between my hatred of the empire I served and my rage against the evil-spirited little beasts who tried to make my job impossible. With one part of my mind I thought of the British Raj[5] as an unbreakable tyranny, as something clamped down, *in saecula saeculorum*[6], upon the will of **prostrate** peoples; with another part I thought that the greatest joy in the world would be to drive a bayonet into a Buddhist priest's guts. Feelings like these are the normal by-products of imperialism; ask any Anglo-Indian official, if you can catch him off duty.

3   One day something happened which in a roundabout way was enlightening. It was a tiny incident in itself, but it gave me a better glimpse than I had had before of the real nature of imperialism— the real motives for which despotic governments act. Early one morning the sub-inspector at a police station the other end of the town rang me up on the phone and said that an elephant was ravaging the bazaar. Would I please come and do something about it? I did not know what I could do, but I wanted to see what was happening and I got on to a pony and started out. I took my rifle, an old .44 Winchester and much too small to kill an elephant, but I thought the noise might be useful *in terrorem*[7]. Various Burmans stopped me on the way and told me about the elephant's doings. It was not, of course, a wild elephant, but a tame one which had gone "must." It had been chained up, as tame elephants always are when their attack of "must" is due, but on the previous night it had broken its chain and escaped. Its mahout, the only person who could manage it when it was in that state, had set out in pursuit, but had taken the wrong direction and was now twelve hours' journey away, and in the morning the elephant had suddenly reappeared in the town. The Burmese population had no weapons and were quite helpless against it. It had already destroyed somebody's bamboo hut, killed a cow and raided some fruit-stalls and devoured the stock; also it had met the municipal rubbish van and, when the driver jumped out and took to his heels, had turned the van over and inflicted violences upon it.

Skill:
Author's Purpose
and Point of View

Orwell's purpose is to tell the truth about imperialism. The repetition of "real" shows he learned something he was trying to convince his readers of, too. This excerpt works because Orwell makes his intentions clear.

5. **the British Raj** the administration of the British Empire in colonial India, which consisted of the modern states of India, Pakistan, Afghanistan, Bangladesh and Myanmar (Burma) from 1858 to 1947
6. *in saecula saeculorum* a Latin phrase from the New Testament meaning "forever and ever"
7. *in terrorem* from the Latin, a threat or clause compelling someone to withdraw or avoid action

NOTES

4 The Burmese sub-inspector and some Indian constables were waiting for me in the quarter where the elephant had been seen. It was a very poor quarter, a labyrinth of squalid bamboo huts, thatched with palmleaf, winding all over a steep hillside. I remember that it was a cloudy, stuffy morning at the beginning of the rains. We began questioning the people as to where the elephant had gone and, as usual, failed to get any definite information. That is invariably the case in the East; a story always sounds clear enough at a distance, but the nearer you get to the scene of events the vaguer it becomes. Some of the people said that the elephant had gone in one direction, some said that he had gone in another, some professed not even to have heard of any elephant. I had almost made up my mind that the whole story was a pack of lies, when we heard yells a little distance away. There was a loud, scandalized cry of "Go away, child! Go away this instant!" and an old woman with a switch in her hand came round the corner of a hut, violently shooing away a crowd of naked children. Some more women followed, clicking their tongues and exclaiming; evidently there was something that the children ought not to have seen. I rounded the hut and saw a man's dead body sprawling in the mud. He was an Indian, a black Dravidian coolie[8], almost naked, and he could not have been dead many minutes. The people said that the elephant had come suddenly upon him round the corner of the hut, caught him with its trunk, put its foot on his back and ground him into the earth. This was the rainy season and the ground was soft, and his face had scored a trench a foot deep and a couple of yards long. He was lying on his belly with arms crucified and head sharply twisted to one side. His face was coated with mud, the eyes wide open, the teeth bared and grinning with an expression of unendurable agony. (Never tell me, by the way, that the dead look peaceful. Most of the corpses I have seen looked devilish.) The friction of the great beast's foot had stripped the skin from his back as neatly as one skins a rabbit. As soon as I saw the dead man I sent an orderly to a friend's house nearby to borrow an elephant rifle. I had already sent back the pony, not wanting it to go mad with fright and throw me if it smelt the elephant.

Skill:
Figurative Language

Orwell uses a simile here to help readers visualize what the dead man's back looked like. This also has the effect of demeaning the dead man and personifying the elephant, making its actions seem intentional and methodical.

5 The orderly came back in a few minutes with a rifle and five cartridges, and meanwhile some Burmans had arrived and told us that the elephant was in the paddy fields below, only a few hundred yards away. As I started forward practically the whole population of the quarter flocked out of the houses and followed me. They had seen the rifle and were all shouting excitedly that I was going to shoot the elephant. They had not shown much interest in the elephant when he was merely ravaging their homes, but it was different now that he was going to be shot. It was a bit of fun to them, as it would be to an English crowd; besides they wanted the meat. It made me vaguely uneasy. I had no intention of shooting the elephant—I had merely sent for the rifle to defend myself if necessary—and it is always unnerving to have a crowd following you. I marched down the hill, looking and feeling a fool, with the rifle over my shoulder and an ever-growing army of people **jostling** at my heels. At the bottom, when you got

8. **coolie** (derogatory) an indentured laborer

away from the huts, there was a metalled road and beyond that a **miry** waste of paddy fields a thousand yards across, not yet ploughed but soggy from the first rains and dotted with coarse grass. The elephant was standing eight yards from the road, his left side towards us. He took not the slightest notice of the crowd's approach. He was tearing up bunches of grass, beating them against his knees to clean them and stuffing them into his mouth.

6   I had halted on the road. As soon as I saw the elephant I knew with perfect certainty that I ought not to shoot him. It is a serious matter to shoot a working elephant—it is comparable to destroying a huge and costly piece of machinery—and obviously one ought not to do it if it can possibly be avoided. And at that distance, peacefully eating, the elephant looked no more dangerous than a cow. I thought then and I think now that his attack of "must" was already passing off; in which case he would merely wander harmlessly about until the mahout came back and caught him. Moreover, I did not in the least want to shoot him. I decided that I would watch him for a little while to make sure that he did not turn savage again, and then go home.

7   But at that moment I glanced round at the crowd that had followed me. It was an immense crowd, two thousand at the least and growing every minute. It blocked the road for a long distance on either side. I looked at the sea of yellow faces above the garish clothes-faces all happy and excited over this bit of fun, all certain that the elephant was going to be shot. They were watching me as they would watch a conjurer about to perform a trick. They did not like me, but with the magical rifle in my hands I was momentarily worth watching. And suddenly I realized that I should have to shoot the elephant after all. The people expected it of me and I had got to do it; I could feel their two thousand wills pressing me forward, irresistibly. And it was at this moment, as I stood there with the rifle in my hands, that I first grasped the hollowness, the futility of the white man's dominion in the East. Here was I, the white man with his gun, standing in front of the unarmed native crowd—seemingly the leading actor of the piece; but in reality I was only an absurd puppet pushed to and fro by the will of those yellow faces behind. I perceived in this moment that when the white man turns tyrant it is his own freedom that he destroys. He becomes a sort of hollow, posing dummy, the conventionalized figure of a sahib[9]. For it is the condition of his rule that he shall spend his life in trying to impress the "natives," and so in every crisis he has got to do what the "natives" expect of him. He wears a mask, and his face grows to fit it. I had got to shoot the elephant. I had committed myself to doing it when I sent for the rifle. A sahib has got to act like a sahib; he has got to appear resolute, to know his own mind and do definite things. To come all that way, rifle in hand, with two thousand people marching at my heels, and then to trail feebly away, having done nothing—no, that was impossible. The crowd would laugh at me. And my whole life, every white man's life in the East, was one long struggle not to be laughed at.

9. **Sahib** an honorific term used a sign of respect in British India, derived from Arabic, meaning "young prince"

Skill:
Figurative
Language

Here Orwell compares the elephant to two things: machinery and a cow. Like machinery, the elephant is very valuable in Burmese society. And like a cow, the elephant does not appear to be a threat.

Skill:
Connotation
and Denotation

I know condition can mean the state of something, such as how well it functions. While this meaning works here, it seems Orwell is trying to connote or denote another meaning because the previous sentence has a negative tone.

NOTES

8　But I did not want to shoot the elephant. I watched him beating his bunch of grass against his knees, with that preoccupied grandmotherly air that elephants have. It seemed to me that it would be murder to shoot him. At that age I was not squeamish about killing animals, but I had never shot an elephant and never wanted to. (Somehow it always seems worse to kill a large animal.) Besides, there was the beast's owner to be considered. Alive, the elephant was worth at least a hundred pounds; dead, he would only be worth the value of his tusks, five pounds, possibly. But I had got to act quickly. I turned to some experienced-looking Burmans who had been there when we arrived, and asked them how the elephant had been behaving. They all said the same thing: he took no notice of you if you left him alone, but he might charge if you went too close to him.

9　It was perfectly clear to me what I ought to do. I ought to walk up to within, say, twenty-five yards of the elephant and test his behavior. If he charged, I could shoot; if he took no notice of me, it would be safe to leave him until the mahout came back. But also I knew that I was going to do no such thing. I was a poor shot with a rifle and the ground was soft mud into which one would sink at every step. If the elephant charged and I missed him, I should have about as much chance as a toad under a steam-roller. But even then I was not thinking particularly of my own skin, only of the watchful yellow faces behind. For at that moment, with the crowd watching me, I was not afraid in the ordinary sense, as I would have been if I had been alone. A white man mustn't be frightened in front of "natives"; and so, in general, he isn't frightened. The sole thought in my mind was that if anything went wrong those two thousand Burmans would see me pursued, caught, trampled on and reduced to a grinning corpse like that Indian up the hill. And if that happened it was quite probable that some of them would laugh. That would never do.

Skill:
Author's Purpose
and Point of View

I thought he would be most afraid of being "trampled on" by the elephant. Instead, he's more concerned with being humiliated than being killed. This point of view is effective because it is unexpected, which makes it memorable.

10　There was only one alternative. I shoved the cartridges into the magazine and lay down on the road to get a better aim. The crowd grew very still, and a deep, low, happy sigh, as of people who see the theatre curtain go up at last, breathed from innumerable throats. They were going to have their bit of fun after all. The rifle was a beautiful German thing with cross-hair sights. I did not then know that in shooting an elephant one would shoot to cut an imaginary bar running from ear-hole to ear-hole. I ought, therefore, as the elephant was sideways on, to have aimed straight at his ear-hole, actually I aimed several inches in front of this, thinking the brain would be further forward.

11　When I pulled the trigger I did not hear the bang or feel the kick—one never does when a shot goes home—but I heard the devilish roar of glee that went up from the crowd. In that instant, in too short a time, one would have thought, even for the bullet to get there, a mysterious, terrible change had come over the elephant. He neither stirred nor fell, but every line of his body had altered. He looked suddenly stricken, shrunken, immensely old, as though the frightful impact of the bullet had paralysed him without knocking him down. At last, after what seemed a long time —it might have been five seconds, I dare say—he sagged flabbily to his knees. His mouth slobbered. An enormous senility seemed to have settled upon him. One could have imagined him thousands of years old. I fired again into the same spot. At the second shot he did not collapse but climbed with desperate slowness to his feet and stood weakly upright, with legs sagging and head drooping. I fired a third time. That was the shot that did for him. You could see the agony of it jolt his whole body and knock the last remnant of strength from his legs. But in falling he seemed for a moment to rise, for as his hind legs collapsed beneath him he seemed to tower upward like a huge rock toppling, his trunk reaching skyward like a tree. He trumpeted, for the first and only time. And then down he came, his belly towards me, with a crash that seemed to shake the ground even where I lay.

12   I got up. The Burmans were already racing past me across the mud. It was obvious that the elephant would never rise again, but he was not dead. He was breathing very rhythmically with long rattling gasps, his great mound of a side painfully rising and falling. His mouth was wide open—I could see far down into caverns of pale pink throat. I waited a long time for him to die, but his breathing did not weaken. Finally I fired my two remaining shots into the spot where I thought his heart must be. The thick blood welled out of him like red velvet, but still he did not die. His body did not even jerk when the shots hit him, the tortured breathing continued without a pause. He was dying, very slowly and in great agony, but in some world remote from me where not even a bullet could damage him further. I felt that I had got to put an end to that dreadful noise. It seemed dreadful to see the great beast lying there, powerless to move and yet powerless to die, and not even to be able to finish him. I sent back for my small rifle and poured shot after shot into his heart and down his throat. They seemed to make no impression. The tortured gasps continued as steadily as the ticking of a clock.

13   In the end I could not stand it any longer and went away. I heard later that it took him half an hour to die. Burmans were bringing dahs and baskets even before I left, and I was told they had stripped his body almost to the bones by the afternoon.

14   Afterwards, of course, there were endless discussions about the shooting of the elephant. The owner was furious, but he was only an Indian and could do nothing. Besides, legally I had done the right thing, for a mad elephant has to be killed, like a mad dog, if its owner fails to control it. Among the Europeans opinion was divided. The older men said I was right, the younger men said it was a damn shame to shoot an elephant for killing a coolie, because an elephant was worth more than any damn Coringhee coolie[10]. And afterwards I was very glad that the coolie had been killed; it put me legally in the right and it gave me a sufficient **pretext** for shooting the elephant. I often wondered whether any of the others grasped that I had done it solely to avoid looking a fool.

10. **Coringhee coolie** a laborer who has migrated from Southern India, or Coringhee

First Read

Read "Shooting an Elephant." After you read, complete the Think Questions below.

1. According to Orwell, he was "hated by large numbers of people" during his time in Burma. Why was he so hated? Support your answer using textual evidence.

2. Referring to information that is directly stated or implied, what does Orwell mean when he says he "had to think out my problems in utter silence?"

3. In two or three sentences, explain why Orwell was "very glad" the elephant had killed someone.

4. Use context clues to determine the meaning of the word **oppressors** as it is used in the text. Write your definition of *oppressors* here and explain how you figured it out.

5. Keeping in mind that the Old Norse word *myrr* means "bog" or "swamp," determine the meaning of **miry** as it is used in the text. Write your definition of *miry* here. Then check your inferred meaning in a print or digital library.

Skill: Author's Purpose and Point of View

Use the Checklist to analyze Author's Purpose and Point of View in "Shooting an Elephant." Refer to the sample student annotations about Author's Purpose and Point of View in the text.

••• CHECKLIST FOR AUTHOR'S PURPOSE AND POINT OF VIEW

In order to identify author's purpose and point of view, note the following:

- ✓ whether the writer is attempting to establish trust by citing his or her experience or education

- ✓ whether the evidence the author provides is convincing and that the argument or position is logical

- ✓ what words and phrases the author uses to appeal to the emotions

- ✓ the author's use of rhetoric, or the art of speaking and writing persuasively, such as the use of repetition to drive home a point as well as allusion and alliteration

- ✓ the author's use of rhetoric to contribute to the power, persuasiveness, or beauty of the text

To determine the author's purpose and point of view, consider the following questions:

- ✓ How does the author try to convince me that he or she has something valid and important for me to read?

- ✓ What words or phrases express emotion or invite an emotional response? How or why are they effective or ineffective?

- ✓ What words and phrases contribute to the power, persuasiveness, or beauty of the text? Is the author's use of rhetoric successful? Why or why not?

Please note that excerpts and passages in the StudySync® library and this workbook are intended as touchstones to generate interest in an author's work. The excerpts and passages do not substitute for the reading of entire texts, and StudySync® strongly recommends that students seek out and purchase the whole literary or informational work in order to experience it as the author intended. Links to online resellers are available in our digital library. In addition, complete works may be ordered through an authorized reseller by filling out and returning to StudySync® the order form enclosed in this workbook.

Reading & Writing Companion   103

Skill: Author's Purpose and Point of View

Reread paragraphs 12–14 of "Shooting an Elephant." Then, using the Checklist on the previous page, answer the multiple-choice questions below.

⟳ YOUR TURN

1. Orwell's point of view in paragraphs 12–13 is effective because—

   ○ A. it shows the reader how awful it was to watch the elephant die.

   ○ B. it gets the reader to understand that killing elephants requires great skill.

   ○ C. it explains to the reader why it was essential to kill the elephant.

   ○ D. it invites the reader to share Orwell's excitement upon seeing the elephant.

2. How does the information in Paragraph 14 reinforce Orwell's purpose for writing this text?

   ○ A. Orwell explains how the older and younger European men he talked to had different opinions about his actions.

   ○ B. Orwell explains how he was justified in killing the elephant because its owner had not done a good job of controlling it.

   ○ C. Orwell reinforces the horrible reality of colonialism by reducing the killing of the elephant to being a legal issue.

   ○ D. Orwell reinforces his point that Europeans and Burmans have different opinions on colonialism.

Skill:
Connotation and Denotation

Use the Checklist to analyze Connotation and Denotation in "Shooting an Elephant ." Refer to the sample student annotations about Connotation and Denotation in the text.

••• CHECKLIST FOR CONNOTATION AND DENOTATION

In order to identify the denotative meanings of words, use the following steps:

✓ first, note unfamiliar words and phrases, key words used to describe important individuals, events, or ideas, or words that inspire an emotional reaction

✓ next, determine and note the denotative meaning of words by consulting a reference material such as a dictionary, glossary, or thesaurus

✓ finally, analyze nuances in the meaning of words with similar denotations

To better understand the meaning of words and phrases as they are used in a text, including connotative meanings, use the following questions as a guide:

✓ What is the genre or subject of the text? Based on context, what do you think the meaning of the word is intended to be?

✓ Is your inference the same or different from the dictionary definition?

✓ Does the word create a positive, negative, or neutral emotion?

✓ What synonyms or alternative phrasing help you describe the connotative meaning of the word?

To determine the meaning of words and phrases as they are used in a text, including connotative meanings, use the following questions as a guide:

✓ What is the denotative meaning of the word? Is that denotative meaning correct in context?

✓ What possible positive, neutral, or negative connotations might the word have, depending on context?

✓ What textual evidence signals a particular connotation for the word?

Skill:
Connotation and Denotation

Reread paragraph 8 of "Shooting an Elephant ." Then, using the Checklist on the previous page, answer the multiple-choice questions below.

⟳ YOUR TURN

1. What is the most likely connotation of "preoccupied grandmotherly air"?

   ○ A. Negative: The elephant is being described as annoying.

   ○ B. Positive: The elephant is being described as gentle and caring.

   ○ C. Positive: The elephant is being described as wise and funny.

   ○ D. Neutral: The elephant is being described simply as an animal.

2. What is the most likely reason Orwell uses "beast" to describe the elephant?

   ○ A. Orwell wants to convey that the elephant could still be used to help the villagers.

   ○ B. Orwell wants to convey that the elephant has been terribly mistreated by the mahout.

   ○ C. After personifying the elephant, Orwell is telling the reader that it is still evil.

   ○ D. After personifying the elephant, Orwell is reminding the reader that it is still an animal.

Skill:
Figurative Language

Use the Checklist to analyze Figurative Language in "Shooting an Elephant ." Refer to the sample student annotations about Figurative Language in the text.

••• CHECKLIST FOR FIGURATIVE LANGUAGE

In order to determine the meaning of figurative language in context, note the following:

✓ words that mean one thing literally and suggest something else

✓ similes, metaphors, or personification

✓ figures of speech, including

• paradoxes, or a seemingly contradictory statement that when further investigated or explained proves to be true, such as

> a character described as "a wise fool"

> a character stating, "I must be cruel to be kind"

• hyperbole, or exaggerated statements not meant to be taken literally, such as

> a child saying, "I'll be doing this homework until I'm 100!"

> a claim such as, "I'm so hungry I could eat a horse!"

In order to interpret figurative language in context and analyze its role in the text, consider the following questions:

✓ Where is there figurative language in the text and what seems to be the purpose of the author's use of it?

✓ Why does the author use a figure of speech rather than literal language?

✓ What impact does exaggeration or hyperbole have on your understanding of the text?

✓ Where are there examples of paradoxes and how do they affect the meaning in the text?

✓ Which phrases contain references that seem contradictory?

✓ Where are contradictory words and phrases used to enhance the reader's understanding of the character, object, or idea?

✓ How does the figurative language develop the message or theme of the literary work?

Skill:
Figurative Language

Reread paragraph 7 of "Shooting an Elephant ." Then, using the Checklist on the previous page, answer the multiple-choice questions below.

⟳ YOUR TURN

1. What is the best explanation of the simile "as they would watch a conjurer about to perform a trick"?

   ○ A. The Burmese people are treating this experience as a kind of entertainment.
   ○ B. The Burmese people are hoping that Orwell will make the elephant disappear.
   ○ C. The Burmese people believe that Orwell is a kind of magician.
   ○ D. The Burmese people believe that rifles are magical tools.

2. This question has two parts. First, answer Part A. Then, answer Part B.

   Part A: What does the figurative language in this paragraph indicate the speaker is feeling at this moment?

   ○ A. The speaker feels that the elephant is in complete control of the situation and is about to attack him.
   ○ B. The speaker feels that he has lost control of the situation and is about to be attacked by the Burmese people.
   ○ C. The speaker feels that the situation is in his control rather than in the control of the Burmese people.
   ○ D. The speaker feels that the situation is in the control of the Burmese people rather than in his control.

   Part B: Which simile or metaphor best supports your answer to Part A?

   ○ A. ". . . with the magical rifle in my hands I was momentarily worth watching."
   ○ B. ". . . the futility of the white man's dominion in the East."
   ○ C. "Here was I, the white man with his gun, standing in front of the unarmed native crowd . . ."
   ○ D. "I was only an absurd puppet pushed to and fro by the will of those yellow faces behind."

Close Read

Reread "Shooting an Elephant." As you reread, complete the Skills Focus questions below. Then use your answers and annotations from the questions to help you complete the Write activity.

◎ SKILLS FOCUS

1. Highlight a passage in which Orwell describes the moral dilemma he is facing. Summarize the dilemma and what it reveals about the theme.

2. Identify a passage in Paragraph 2 in which Orwell describes his strong negative feelings toward both imperialism and the Burmese people. Explain how Orwell's use of language in this passage adds to the effectiveness of the text.

3. Find a section of the text in which the elephant serves as a symbol or metaphor for something else. Explain what the elephant symbolizes.

4. In Paragraph 11, highlight a description of the elephant after Orwell has shot it. Explain the point of view the author is conveying in this passage; then evaluate the effectiveness of the description in communicating that point of view.

5. Throughout the essay, Orwell describes ways in which he feels alienated and separate from everyone around him. Highlight two examples of this, and explain what is causing his alienation.

✏ WRITE

EXPLANATORY ESSAY: What do you think is the point of view Orwell is expressing in his essay "Shooting an Elephant"? Analyze the literary elements and figurative language in the text to determine the author's point of view. Then write a short essay, responding to this question. Remember to use textual evidence to support your response.

Extended
Writing
Project and
Grammar

EXTENDED
WRITING
PROJECT
LITERARY ANALYSIS
WRITING

Literary Analysis Writing Process: Plan

PLAN	DRAFT	REVISE	EDIT AND PUBLISH

At first glance, a poem about an indecisive man, a short story about a woman wearing a new dress, and an essay about shooting an elephant might not seem to have much in common. However, each of these selections is an example of Modernist literature that features themes relating to isolation and alienation.

WRITING PROMPT

Why is alienation such a common theme in Modernist literature?

Consider all the texts you have read in this unit, and reflect on how alienation impacts those who experience it. Then, select three characters or speakers from the texts. Write a literary analysis essay to examine how the authors explore the theme of alienation through these three characters or speakers. In your conclusion, synthesize the ideas in these texts about alienation in the modern world. Regardless of which selections you choose, be sure your literary analysis includes the following:

- an introduction
- a thesis statement
- coherent body paragraphs
- reasons and relevant evidence
- a conclusion

Please note that excerpts and passages in the StudySync® library and this workbook are intended as touchstones to generate interest in an author's work. The excerpts and passages do not substitute for the reading of entire texts, and StudySync® strongly recommends that students seek out and purchase the whole literary or informational work in order to experience it as the author intended. Links to online resellers are available in our digital library. In addition, complete works may be ordered through an authorized reseller by filling out and returning to StudySync® the order form enclosed in this workbook.

Reading & Writing Companion

111

Introduction to Literary Analysis Writing

A literary analysis is a form of argumentative writing that tries to persuade readers to accept the writer's interpretation of a literary text. Good literary analysis writing builds an argument with a strong claim, convincing reasons, relevant textual evidence, and a clear structure with an introduction, body, and conclusion. The characteristics of literary analysis writing include:

- an introduction
- a thesis statement
- textual evidence
- transitions
- a formal style
- a conclusion

In addition to these characteristics, writers of literary analyses also carefully craft their work through their use of a strong, confident tone and compelling syntax, or sentence structure, which help to make the text more persuasive. Effective arguments combine these genre characteristics and elements of the writer's craft to engage and convince the reader.

As you continue with this Extended Writing Project, you'll receive more instruction and practice in crafting each of the characteristics of literary analysis writing to create your own literary analysis.

Before you get started on your own literary analysis, read this literary analysis that one student, Emma, wrote in response to the writing prompt. As you read the Model, highlight and annotate the features of literary analysis writing that Emma included in her literary analysis.

☰ STUDENT MODEL

NOTES

Alienation in a Post-War Society

1   In the early 20th century, the world was in flux. New technology led to destruction as war raged in Europe. At the same time, many challenged traditional norms of gender and class. For example, women's suffrage movements gained traction in both Great Britain and the United States. The world people thought they knew was changing, and as a result men and women of all levels of society felt lost. Writers and artists reacted by challenging old conventions and social norms. They created new styles and sought to represent individuals' subjective points of view. Alienation is a common theme in modernist literature because uncertainty was a by-product of the rapidly changing society. Modernist works such as "The Love Song of J. Alfred Prufrock," "The New Dress," and "A Cup of Tea" show that feelings of alienation stretched across lines of gender and class.

2   Although he was born in the United States, poet T. S. Eliot moved to England in 1914 while World War I raged in Europe. His poem "The Love Song of J. Alfred Prufrock," published the following year, reflects the disillusionment and uncertainty Europeans felt as the world changed around them. The first images in the poem create tension as a familiar scene turns ominous: "Let us go then, you and I, / When the evening is spread out against the sky / Like a patient etherized upon a table" (7–9). An evening stroll under the night sky is typically a romantic or serene image, but Eliot uses it differently. By comparing the evening to a patient about to have surgery, Eliot upends expectations. This makes readers uncomfortable because they do not know what will happen on the journey on which they are about to embark with the poem's speaker.

3   Uncertainty and alienation are also reflected in the speaker himself. He constantly doubts his own worth and place in the world. Instead of simply interacting with people, he stops to ask, "Do I dare / Disturb the universe?" (51–52). The entire poem takes place in the speaker's

own mind. There are no outside forces preventing him from engaging with others. The speaker's own hesitancy and insecurity prevent him from participating in society. In this way, "The Love Song of J. Alfred Prufrock" shows that alienation can be a product of our own making.

4   The protagonist of Virginia Woolf's short story "The New Dress" is also a victim of her own insecurities. Like the speaker of Eliot's poem, Mabel Waring wants to participate in society but is instead alienated by her own feelings of inadequacy. Mabel is so worried that the other guests will judge her that she cannot enjoy herself at a party:

> And at once the misery which she always tried to hide, the profound dissatisfaction—the sense she had had, ever since she was a child, of being inferior to other people—set upon her, relentlessly, remorselessly, with an intensity which she could not beat off, as she would when she woke at night at home, by reading Borrow or Scott; for oh these men, oh these women, all were thinking—"What's Mabel wearing? What a fright she looks! What a hideous new dress!"—their eyelids flickering as they came up and then their lids shutting rather tight. It was her own appalling inadequacy; her cowardice; her mean, water-sprinkled blood that depressed her.

Mabel's uncertainty is directly tied to her perception of society's expectations. She worries that, as a member of a slightly lower social class, she cannot measure up to other guests' expectations, and it makes her doubt her worth. Later, when a fellow party guest points out that Mabel has bought a new dress, it causes her to unravel: "'Why,' she asked herself, 'can't I . . . feel sure about the canary and pity and love and not be whipped all round in a second by coming into a room full of people?'" Instead of enjoying her social interactions, Mabel allows a single comment to send her into a spiral of anxiety and shame. In the end, she leaves the party early, too embarrassed by her appearance to remain in the company of others. "The New Dress" shows that alienation can be a product of society's expectations.

5   Rosemary Fell, the protagonist in Katherine Mansfield's "A Cup of Tea," is the opposite of Mabel in several key ways. Rosemary is a member of London's high society and is extremely wealthy. She is also well-respected and sure of her place in the world. Yet, Rosemary

also fails to connect with the people around her. When she decides to invite a penniless young woman, Miss Smith, home for tea, she does so in order to make herself feel like a benefactor instead of out of a genuine desire to make a friend: "She was going to prove to this girl that—wonderful things did happen in life, that—fairy godmothers were real, that—rich people had hearts, and that women *were* sisters." The class difference between the characters prevents Rosemary from seeing Miss Smith as a whole person. Instead, she views the interaction as a game to keep herself entertained on a rainy day. This becomes clear when she abruptly throws Miss Smith out after her husband, Philip, comments on the young woman's beauty. Just as the guest's comment affects Mabel in "The New Dress," this passing commentary sends Rosemary into a spiral as the words echo in her head: "Pretty! Absolutely lovely! Bowled over! Her heart beat like a heavy bell." Rosemary abandons Miss Smith at the first sign that their friendship could lead to a rivalry for her husband's attention. Later, Rosemary asks her husband to reassure her. "'Philip,' she whispered, and she pressed his head against her bosom, 'am I *pretty*?'" As the story concludes, Miss Smith has been alienated by the woman who claimed to be her benefactor, and Rosemary feels insecure in her relationship with her husband. "A Cup of Tea" shows that alienation can occur when issues relating to class and gender complicate individual relationships between two people.

6 The characters in these modernist works come from different backgrounds and have different experiences, but the results of their attempted interactions with others are similar. Hindered by their own insecurities, the speaker in "The Love Song of J. Alfred Prufrock" and the protagonists in "The New Dress" and "A Cup of Tea" are left alone and afraid. Alienation is a common theme in these modernist works because in a post-war, ever-changing world, it is human nature to ask, "Am I good enough?"

Please note that excerpts and passages in the StudySync® library and this workbook are intended as touchstones to generate interest in an author's work. The excerpts and passages do not substitute for the reading of entire texts, and StudySync® strongly recommends that students seek out and purchase the whole literary or informational work in order to experience it as the author intended. Links to online resellers are available in our digital library. In addition, complete works may be ordered through an authorized reseller by filling out and returning to StudySync® the order form enclosed in this workbook.

Reading & Writing Companion   115

✎ WRITE

Writers often take notes about their ideas for a literary analysis before they sit down to write. Think about what you've learned so far about literary analysis writing to help you begin prewriting.

- **Purpose:** What selections do you want to write about, and how do they develop themes relating to alienation?

- **Audience:** Who is your audience, and what idea do you want to express to them?

- **Introduction:** How will you introduce your topic? How will you engage an audience and preview what you plan to argue in your essay?

- **Thesis Statement:** What is your claim about the selections you've chosen? How can you word your claim so it is clear to readers?

- **Textual Evidence:** What evidence will you use to support your claim? What facts, details, examples, and quotations will persuade your audience to agree with your claim?

- **Transitions:** How will you smoothly transition from one idea to another within and across paragraphs?

- **Formal Style:** How can you create and maintain a formal style and an objective tone as you build your argument?

- **Conclusion:** How will you wrap up your argument? How can you restate the main ideas in your argument without being redundant?

Response Instructions

Use the questions in the bulleted list to write a one-paragraph summary. Your summary should describe what you will argue in your literary analysis.

Don't worry about including all of the details now; focus only on the most essential and important elements. You will refer to this short summary as you continue through the steps of the writing process.

Skill: Reasons and Relevant Evidence

••• CHECKLIST FOR REASONS AND RELEVANT EVIDENCE

As you determine the reasons and relevant evidence you will need to support your claim, use the following questions as a guide:

- What is my claim (or claims)? What are the strengths and limitations of my claim(s)?

- What relevant evidence do I have? Where could I add more support for my claim(s)?

- What do I know about the audience's:

  > knowledge about my topic?

  > concerns and values?

  > possible biases toward the subject matter?

Use the following steps to help you develop claims fairly and thoroughly:

- establish a claim. Then, evaluate:

  > its strengths and limitations

  > any biases you have

  > any gaps in support for your claim, so that your support can be more thorough

- consider your audience and their perspective on your topic. Determine:

  > their probable prior knowledge about the topic

  > their concerns and values

  > any biases they may have toward the subject matter

- find the most relevant evidence that supports the claim

YOUR TURN

Read the quotations from "A Cup of Tea" below. Then, complete the chart by sorting the quotations into two categories: those that serve as relevant evidence to support Emma's claim and those that do not. Write the corresponding letter for each quotation in the appropriate column.

	Quotations
A	"Rosemary had been married two years. She had a duck of a boy. No, not Peter—Michael. And her husband absolutely adored her."
B	"Half an hour later Philip was still in the library, when Rosemary came in."
C	"Rosemary Fell was not exactly beautiful. No, you couldn't have called her beautiful. Pretty? Well, if you took her to pieces. . . But why be so cruel as to take anyone to pieces?"
D	"'Do you like me?' said she, and her tone, sweet, husky, troubled him."
E	"She went to her writing-room and sat down at her desk. Pretty! Absolutely lovely! Bowled over! Her heart beat like a heavy bell."
F	"The other did stop just in time for Rosemary to get up before the tea came. She had the table placed between them."

Supports Claim	Does Not Support Claim

WRITE

Use the questions in the checklist to draft your claim and select reasons and relevant evidence for your argumentative literary analysis essay.

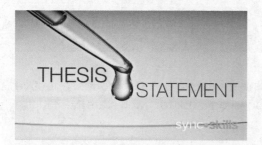

Skill:
Thesis Statement

••• CHECKLIST FOR THESIS STATEMENT

Before you begin writing your thesis statement, ask yourself the following questions:

- What is the prompt asking me to write about?
- What claim do I want to make about the topic of this essay?
- Is my claim precise and informative?
- How is my claim specific to my topic? How does it inform the reader about my topic?
- Does my thesis statement introduce the body of my essay?
- Where should I place my thesis statement?

Here are some methods for introducing and developing a topic as well as a precise and informative claim:

- think about your central claim of your essay
  - > identify a clear claim you want to introduce, thinking about:
    - o how closely your claim is related to your topic and how specific it is to your supporting details
    - o how your claim includes necessary information to guide the reader through the topic
  - > identify as many claims as you intend to prove
- your thesis statement should:
  - > let the reader anticipate the content of your essay
  - > help you begin your essay in an organized manner
  - > present your opinion clearly
  - > respond completely to the writing prompt
- consider the best placement for your thesis statement
  - > if your response is short, you may want to present your thesis statement in the first sentence of the essay
  - > if your response is longer (as in a formal essay), you can place it at the end of your introductory paragraph

YOUR TURN

Read the thesis statements below. Then, complete the chart by sorting them into two categories: effective thesis statements and ineffective thesis statements. Write the corresponding letter for each statement in the appropriate column.

Thesis Statements	
A	"The New Dress" and "A Cup of Tea" both offer harsh criticism of traditional gender roles.
B	In *A Room of One's Own,* Virginia Woolf argues that women have been negatively affected by unfair limitations.
C	"The New Dress" and "A Cup of Tea" were both written by women in the early 20th century.
D	Virginia Woolf's *A Room of One's Own* includes a long passage that hypothesizes about what might have happened if Shakespeare had had an equally talented sister.
E	T. S. Eliot's "The Love Song of J. Alfred Prufrock" is a difficult poem for most readers to understand.
F	T. S. Eliot's poem "The Love Song of J. Alfred Prufrock" warns readers that time is fleeting.

Effective Thesis Statements	Ineffective Thesis Statements

✏️ **WRITE**

Use the questions in the checklist to plan and write your thesis statement.

Skill: Organizing Argumentative Writing

••• CHECKLIST FOR ORGANIZING ARGUMENTATIVE WRITING

As you consider how to organize your writing for your argumentative essay, use the following questions as a guide:

• What kinds of evidence could I find that would support my claim?

• Did I choose an organizational structure that establishes clear relationships between claims and supporting reasons and evidence?

Follow these steps to organize your argumentative essay in a way that logically sequences claim(s), reasons, and evidence:

• identify your precise, or specific, claim or claims and the evidence that supports them

• establish the significance of your claim

> find what others may have written about the topic, and learn why they feel it is important

> look for possible consequences or complications if something is done or is not accomplished

• choose an organizational structure that logically sequences and establishes clear relationships among claims, opposing claims or counterclaims, and the evidence presented to support the claims

↻ YOUR TURN

Read the thesis statements below. Then, complete the chart by writing the organizational structure that would be most appropriate for the purpose, topic, and context of the corresponding essay, as well as the audience.

Organizational Structure Options		
order of importance	cause and effect	compare and contrast

Thesis Statement	Organizational Structure
The devastation of the world wars led to a sense of isolation among authors and readers.	
Modernists had more in common with Victorian writers than one might think.	
Many factors led Romantics to idolize nature, but the Industrial Revolution had the strongest influence.	

↻ YOUR TURN

Complete the outline by writing an introductory statement, thesis statement, and three main ideas as well as supporting evidence for the body paragraphs of your argumentative essay. Make sure your ideas are appropriate for the purpose, topic, and context of your essay, as well as your audience.

Outline	Summary
Introductory Statement	
Thesis	
Body Paragraph 1	
Supporting Evidence 1	
Body Paragraph 2	
Supporting Evidence 2	
Body Paragraph 3	
Supporting Evidence 3	

Literary Analysis Writing Process: Draft

PLAN	DRAFT	REVISE	EDIT AND PUBLISH

You have already made progress toward writing your literary analysis. Now it is time to draft your literary analysis.

✏ WRITE

Use your plan and other responses in your Binder to draft your literary analysis. You may also have new ideas as you begin drafting. Feel free to explore those new ideas as you have them. You can also ask yourself these questions to ensure that your writing is focused and organized and has appropriate evidence and elaboration to support your thesis:

Draft Checklist:

☐ **Purpose and Focus:** Have I made my topic and claim clear to readers? Have I included only relevant information and details and nothing extraneous that might confuse my readers?

☐ **Organization:** Is the organizational structure of my essay appropriate for my purpose, audience, topic, and context? Are my ideas presented in a way that persuades readers?

☐ **Evidence and Elaboration:** Will my readers be able to easily understand the connection between my ideas and supporting evidence?

Before you submit your draft, read it over carefully. You want to be sure that you've responded to all aspects of the prompt.

Here is Emma's literary analysis draft. As you read, notice how Emma develops her draft to be focused and organized, so it has relevant evidence and elaboration to support her ideas. As she continues to revise and edit her literary analysis, she will find and improve weak spots in her writing, as well as correct any language or punctuation mistakes.

NOTES

STUDENT MODEL: FIRST DRAFT

Alienation in a Post-War Society

~~In the early 20th century, the world was in flux. The world people thought they knew was changing, and as a result men and women of all levels of society felt lost. Old conventions and social norms were challenged by writers and artists. They created new styles, and these same writers and artists sought to represent individuals' subjective points of view. "The Love Song of J. Alfred Prufrock," "The New Dress," and "A Cup of Tea" show that feelings of alienation can affect anyone.~~

In the early 20th century, the world was in flux. New technology led to destruction as war raged in Europe. At the same time, many challenged traditional norms of gender and class. For example, women's suffrage movements gained traction in both Great Britain and the United States. The world people thought they knew was changing, and as a result men and women of all levels of society felt lost. Writers and artists reacted by challenging old conventions and social norms. They created new styles and sought to represent individuals' subjective points of view. Alienation is a common theme in modernist literature because uncertainty was a by-product of the rapidly changing society. Modernist works such as "The Love Song of J. Alfred Prufrock," "The New Dress," and "A Cup of Tea" show that feelings of alienation stretched across lines of gender and class.

Poet T. S. Eliot moved to England in 1914 while World War I was going on in Europe. Although he was born in the United States. T. S. Eliot's poem "The Love Song of J. Alfred Prufrock," published in 1915, reflects the uncertainty Europeans felt as the world changed around them. The first images in the poem create tension as a familiar scene turns ominous:

> Let us go then, you and I,
> When the evening is spread out against the sky
> Like a patient etherized upon a table.

Skill:
Introductions

Emma decides to provide more context in the beginning of her introduction by adding details to show why the world was changing. She then adds a sentence about alienation to connect her introductory sentences and her thesis statement. Finally, she rephrases her thesis to give her essay a more precise focus.

An evening stroll under the night sky is typically a romantic or serene image, but Eliot uses it differently. By comparing the evening to a patient about to have surgery, Eliot goes against the reader's expectations for how natural imagery will work in the poem. This makes readers uncomfortable because they do not know what will happen on the journey on which they are about to embarck with him. Uncertainty and alienation are apparent in the speaker himself. He constantly doubts his own worth and place in the world. Instead of simply interacting with people, he stops to ask: Do I dare Disturb the universe? The entire poem takes place in the speaker's own mind. Because of insecurity, the speaker struggles to participate in society. In this way, "The Love Song of J. Alfred Prufrock" shows that alienation can be a product of our own making.

The person in Virginia Woolf's short story is also a victim of insecurities, like the speaker of Eliot's poem, she wants to participate in society but is instead alienated by her own feelings of inadequacy. In "The New Dress," Mabel Waring is so worried that the other guests will judge her that she cannot enjoy herself at a party:

> And at once the misery which she always tried to hide, the profound dissatisfaction—the sense she had had, ever since she was a child, of being inferior to other people—set upon her, relentlessly, remorselessly, with an intensity which she could not beat off, as she would when she woke at night at home, by reading Borrow or Scott; for oh these men, oh these women, all were thinking—"What's Mabel wearing? What a fright she looks! What a hideous new dress!"—their eyelids flickering as they came up and then their lids shutting rather tight. It was her own appalling inadequacy; her cowardice; her mean, water-sprinkled blood that depressed her.

Later, when a fellow party guest points out that Mabel has bought a new dress, it causes her to unravel. Instead of enjoying her social interactions, Mabel allows a single comment to send her into a spiral of anxiety and shame. In the end, she leaves the party early, too embarrassed by her appearance to remain in the company of others. "The New Dress" is a story about society's expectations.

Rosemary Fell, the protagonist in Katherine Mansfield's "A Cup of Tea" is a member of London's high society and is extremely wealthy.

Skill:
Transitions

To connect her
discussion of the two
stories, Emma focuses
on how the authors
approach the same
theme from different
perspectives. She
modifies the concluding
sentence of her
paragraph about "The
New Dress" to
summarize her analysis
of this theme in the
story. She then creates
a transition to her
discussion of "A Cup of
Tea" by contrasting the
two protagonists in her
new topic sentence
about that work.

She is also well-respected and sure of her place in the world. Yet, Rosemary also fails to connect with the people around her. When she decides to invite a penniless young woman home for tea, she does so in order to make herself feel like a benefactor instead of out of a genuine desire to make a friend. Rosemary is kept from seeing Miss Smith as a whole person by the class difference. Instead, she views the interaction as a game to keep herself entertained on a rainy day, which becomes clear when she abruptly throws Miss Smith out after husband, Philip, comments on the young woman's beauty. Like Mabel's experience, this sends Rosemary into a spiral as the words echo in her head, "Pretty! Absolutely lovely! Bowled over! Her heart beat like a heavy bell." Rosemary asks her husband to reassure her. "'Philip,' she whispered, and she pressed his head against her bosom, 'am I pretty?'" Rosemary abandons Miss Smith at the first sign of that their friendship could lead to a rivalry for her husband's attention. Miss Smith has been alienated by the woman who claimed to be her benefactor, and Rosemary feels insecure in her relationship with her husband.

The protagonist of Virginia Woolf's short story "The New Dress" is also a victim of her own insecurities. Like the speaker of Eliot's poem, Mabel Waring wants to participate in society but is instead alienated by her own feelings of inadequacy. Mabel is so worried that the other guests will judge her that she cannot enjoy herself at a party:

> And at once the misery which she always tried to hide, the profound dissatisfaction—the sense she had had, ever since she was a child, of being inferior to other people—set upon her, relentlessly, remorselessly, with an intensity which she could not beat off, as she would when she woke at night at home, by reading Borrow or Scott; for oh these men, oh these women, all were thinking—"What's Mabel wearing? What a fright she looks! What a hideous new dress!"—their eyelids flickering as they came up and then their lids shutting rather tight. It was her own appalling inadequacy; her cowardice; her mean, water-sprinkled blood that depressed her.

Mabel's uncertainty is directly tied to her perception of society's expectations. She worries that, as a member of a slightly lower social class, she cannot measure up to other guests' expectations, and it makes her doubt her worth. Later, when a fellow party guest points out that Mabel has bought a new dress, it causes her to unravel: "'Why,' she asked herself, 'can't I . . . feel sure about the canary and pity and love and not be whipped all round in a second by coming into a room full of people?'" Instead of enjoying her social interactions, Mabel allows a single comment to send her into a spiral of anxiety and shame. In the end, she leaves the party early, too embarrassed by her appearance to remain in the company of others. "The New Dress" shows that alienation can be a product of society's expectations.

Rosemary Fell, the protagonist in Katherine Mansfield's "A Cup of Tea," is the opposite of Mabel in several key ways. Rosemary is a member of London's high society and is extremely wealthy. She is also well-respected and sure of her place in the world. Yet, Rosemary also fails to connect with the people around her. When she decides to invite a penniless young woman, Miss Smith, home for tea, she does so in order to make herself feel like a benefactor instead of out of a genuine desire to make a friend: "She was going to prove to this girl that—wonderful things did happen in life, that fairy godmothers were real, that—rich people had hearts, and that women *were* sisters." The class difference between the characters prevents Rosemary from seeing Miss Smith as a whole person. Instead, she views the interaction as a game to keep herself entertained on a rainy day. This becomes clear when she abruptly throws Miss Smith out after her husband, Philip, comments on the young woman's beauty. Just as the guest's comment affects Mabel in "The New Dress," this passing commentary sends Rosemary into a spiral as the words echo in her head: "Pretty! Absolutely lovely! Bowled over! Her heart beat like a heavy bell." Rosemary abandons Miss Smith at the first sign that their friendship could lead to a rivalry for her husband's attention. Later, Rosemary asks her husband to reassure her. "'Philip,' she whispered, and she pressed his head against her bosom, 'am I *pretty*?'" As the story concludes, Miss Smith has been alienated by the woman who claimed to be her benefactor, and Rosemary feels insecure in her relationship with her husband. "A Cup of Tea" shows that alienation can occur when issues relating to class and gender complicate individual relationships between two people.

"The Love Song of J. Alfred Prufrock," "The New Dress," and "A Cup of Tea" prove that feelings of alienation were common during

Please note that excerpts and passages in the StudySync® library and this workbook are intended as touchstones to generate interest in an author's work. The excerpts and passages do not substitute for the reading of entire texts, and StudySync® strongly recommends that students seek out and purchase the whole literary or informational work in order to experience it as the author intended. Links to online resellers are available in our digital library. In addition, complete works may be ordered through an authorized reseller by filling out and returning to StudySync® the order form enclosed in this workbook.

Reading & Writing Companion   127

NOTES

Skill:
Conclusions

Emma strengthens her conclusion by revising the beginning and end of the paragraph. She rephrases her thesis in the first sentence. Then she adds a closing question, which helps her connect with her audience and make her idea memorable.

Modernism. ~~Bewildered by their own feelings, the speaker in "The Love Story of J. Alfred Prufrock" and the protagonists in "The New Dress" and "A Cup of Tea" are left alone and afraid. Alienation is a common theme in these modernist works because in a post-war, ever-changing world art, gender, and class needed redefining.~~

The characters in these modernist works come from different backgrounds and have different experiences, but the results of their attempted interactions with others are similar. Hindered by their own insecurities, the speaker in "The Love Song of J. Alfred Prufrock" and the protagonists in "The New Dress" and "A Cup of Tea" are left alone and afraid. Alienation is a common theme in these modernist works because in a post-war, ever-changing world, it is human nature to ask, "Am I good enough?"

Skill:
Introductions

••• CHECKLIST FOR INTRODUCTIONS

Before you write your introduction, ask yourself the following questions:

- What is my claim? In addition:

  > How can I make it more precise and informative?

  > Have I included why my claim is significant to discuss? How does it help the reader understand the topic better? What does it contribute to the conversation on my topic?

- How can I introduce my topic? Have I organized complex ideas, concepts, and information so that each new element builds on the previous element and creates a unified whole?

- How will I "hook" my reader's interest? I might:

  > start with an attention-grabbing statement

  > begin with an intriguing question

  > use descriptive words to set a scene

Here are two strategies to help you introduce your precise claim and topic clearly in an introduction:

- Peer Discussion

  > Talk about your topic with a partner, explaining what you already know and your ideas about your topic.

  > Write notes about the ideas you have discussed and any new questions you may have.

  > Review your notes, and think about what your claim or controlling idea will be.

  > Briefly state your precise and informative claim, establishing why it is important—or what ideas you are contributing to your topic—and how it is different from other claims about your topic.

  > Write a possible "hook."

- Freewriting

  > Freewrite for 10 minutes about your topic. Don't worry about grammar, punctuation, or having fully formed ideas. The point of freewriting is to discover ideas.

  > Review your notes, and think about what your claim or controlling idea will be.

  > Briefly state your precise and informative claim, establishing why it is important—or what ideas you are contributing to your topic—and how it is different from other claims about your topic.

  > Write a possible "hook."

YOUR TURN

Choose the best answer to the question.

Below is a passage from a previous draft of Emma's introduction. The underlined sentence is inappropriate for the context of an academic essay and does not clearly introduce the topic of the paper. How should Emma revise the sentence to better suit the topic and context?

> <u>Feeling alienated is the worst.</u> Imagine going to a party and being ridiculed by the other guests because you are wearing a new dress, or having your husband tell you that your new friend is more beautiful than you are. How would that make you feel? Alienation is a common theme in modernist literature because writers began to fight back against the unfair social restrictions set on women during this time.

○ A. Women in the early 20th century faced criticism if they did not conform to societal expectations.

○ B. Virginia Woolf and Katherine Mansfield were Modernist writers who examined societal expectations.

○ C. Feeling like an outsider can be a real bummer, and this was a very common feeling for Modernist women.

○ D. Society is way more critical of women than of men, and this was definitely on Virginia Woolf's mind.

WRITE

Use the questions in the checklist to revise the introduction of your literary analysis essay.

Please note that excerpts and passages in the StudySync® library and this workbook are intended as touchstones to generate interest in an author's work. The excerpts and passages do not substitute for the reading of entire texts, and StudySync® strongly recommends that students seek out and purchase the whole literary or informational work in order to experience it as the author intended. Links to online resellers are available in our digital library. In addition, complete works may be ordered through an authorized reseller by filling out and returning to StudySync® the order form enclosed in this workbook.

Reading & Writing Companion   131

Skill:
Transitions

••• CHECKLIST FOR TRANSITIONS

Before you revise your current draft to include transitions, think about:

- the key ideas you discuss in your body paragraphs
- the relationships among your claim(s), reasons, and evidence
- the logical progression of your argument

Next, reread your current draft and note places in your essay where:

- the relationships between your claim(s), reasons, and evidence are unclear
- you could add linking words, vary sentence structure (or syntax), or use other transitional devices to make your argument more cohesive. Look for:

  > sudden jumps in your ideas

  > places where the ideas in a paragraph do not logically follow from the points in the previous paragraph

  > repetitive sentence structures

Revise your draft to use words, phrases, and clauses as well as varied syntax to link the major sections of your essay, create cohesion, and clarify the relationships between claim(s) and reasons and between reasons and evidence, using the following questions as a guide:

- Are there unifying relationships among the claims, reasons, and evidence in my argument?
- Have I clarified these relationships?
- How can I link major sections of my essay using words, phrases, clauses, and varied syntax?

Copyright © BookheadEd Learning, LLC

YOUR TURN

Choose the best answer to each question.

1. Below is a paragraph from a previous draft of Emma's argumentative literary analysis essay. The main idea of the paragraph is unclear. Which sentence should Emma add to the beginning of the paragraph to improve the focus of the paragraph?

> Once she arrives at the party, she cannot stand to look at herself: "But she dared not look in the glass. She could not face the whole horror—the pale yellow, idiotically old-fashioned silk dress with its long skirt and its high sleeves and its waist and all the things that looked so charming in the fashion book, but not on her, not among all these ordinary people." Mabel is very critical of herself.

- ○ A. The main character, Mabel, buys a new dress and goes to a party.
- ○ B. The main character in "The New Dress" is Mabel Waring.
- ○ C. Mabel's internal reflections show that she feels inadequate.
- ○ D. Have you ever felt self-conscious at a party, just like Mabel?

2. Emma wants to improve the transition between two paragraphs in a previous draft of her literary analysis essay by replacing the underlined sentence. Which sentence would be the best transition to include at the beginning of the second paragraph?

> When Mabel's confidence is shaken, she turns to others to buck up her spirits: "one word of affection from Charles would have made all the difference to her at the moment. If he had only said, 'Mabel, you're looking charming to-night!' it would have changed her life." She needs the approval of other people, and whether or not she feels affirmed can deeply impact her mood.
>
> Rosemary Fell, the protagonist of Katherine Mansfield's "A Cup of Tea" is very insecure.

- ○ A. Charles does not respond by giving Mabel a compliment, and this is very similar to what happens in Katherine Mansfield's "A Cup of Tea," which is another Modernist short story.
- ○ B. Even though her economic status is different, Rosemary Fell, the protagonist of Katherine Mansfield's "A Cup of Tea," also feels alienated when she does not feel affirmed by others.
- ○ C. This brief exchange between characters is a pivotal moment in Woolf's short story, so paying close attention to the relationship between Mabel and her husband is very revealing.
- ○ D. The narrator continues, "Charles said nothing of the kind, of course. He was malice itself," emphasizing that Mabel is truly on her own and alienated from even her husband.

✏ **WRITE**

Use the questions in the checklist to revise your use of transitions in a section of your literary analysis essay.

Skill:
Conclusions

••• CHECKLIST FOR CONCLUSIONS

Before you write your conclusion, ask yourself the following questions:

- How can I rephrase the thesis or main idea in my conclusion? What impression can I make on my reader?

- How can I write my conclusion so that it supports and follows logically from my argument?

- How can I conclude with a memorable comment?

Below are two strategies to help you provide a concluding statement or section that follows from and supports your argument:

- Peer Discussion

  > After you have written your introduction and body paragraphs, talk with a partner about what you want readers to remember, writing notes about your discussion.

  > Review your notes, and think about what you wish to express in your conclusion.

  > Do not simply restate your claim or thesis statement. Rephrase your main idea to show the depth of your knowledge and the importance of your claim.

  > Write your conclusion.

- Freewriting

  > Freewrite for 10 minutes about what you might include in your conclusion. Don't worry about grammar, punctuation, or having fully formed ideas. The point of freewriting is to discover ideas.

  > Review your notes, and think about what you wish to express in your conclusion.

  > Do not simply restate your claim or thesis statement. Rephrase your main idea to show the depth of your knowledge and the importance of your claim.

  > Write your conclusion.

YOUR TURN

Choose the best answer to the question.

Below is a passage from a previous draft of Emma's conclusion. She wants to add a sentence to clarify her purpose and leave her audience with a memorable thought. Which sentence should she add?

> Taking a close look at modernist texts shows that doubt and isolation were common feelings during the early 20th century. "The Love Song of J. Alfred Prufrock," "The New Dress," and "A Cup of Tea" reflect how rapid social and political changes made people feel helpless and disconnected at this time in history.

- ○ A. No one likes feeling helpless and disconnected from other people, especially when so much change is happening in the world.
- ○ B. *The Catcher in the Rye* reveals that people still felt this way in the mid-20th century and that the best way to fight this feeling was to find purpose in life.
- ○ C. While isolation was a common feeling, Modernist authors collectively proved that there was nothing left to do but reimagine art, gender, and class.
- ○ D. Modernist authors like T. S. Eliot, Virginia Woolf, and Katherine Mansfield also developed themes that questioned social norms.

 WRITE

Use the questions in the checklist to revise the conclusion of your literary analysis.

Please note that excerpts and passages in the StudySync® library and this workbook are intended as touchstones to generate interest in an author's work. The excerpts and passages do not substitute for the reading of entire texts, and StudySync® strongly recommends that students seek out and purchase the whole literary or informational work in order to experience it as the author intended. Links to online resellers are available in our digital library. In addition, complete works may be ordered through an authorized reseller by filling out and returning to StudySync® the order form enclosed in this workbook.

Reading & Writing
Companion

Literary Analysis Writing Process: Revise

PLAN	DRAFT	REVISE	EDIT AND PUBLISH

You have written a draft of your argumentative literary analysis essay. You have also received input from your peers about how to improve it. Now you are going to revise your draft.

◄◄ REVISION GUIDE

Examine your draft to find areas for revision. Use the guide below to help you review:

Review	Revise	Example
Clarity		
Scan your body paragraphs. Annotate any sentences where the connection between your ideas is unclear.	Add details so the relationship between your ideas is clear.	The entire poem takes place in the speaker's own mind. There are no outside forces preventing him from engaging with others. ~~Because of insecurity, the speaker struggles to participate in society.~~ The speaker's own hesitancy and insecurity prevent him from participating in society.

Review	Revise	Example
Development		
Identify the reasons that support your claims. Annotate places where you feel there is not enough evidence or explanation to support your claims.	Focus on a single idea or claim and add support, such as textual evidence or explanation.	Yet, Rosemary also fails to connect with the people around her. When she decides to invite a penniless young woman, Miss Smith, home for tea, she does so in order to make herself feel like a benefactor instead of out of a genuine desire to make a friend.: "She was going to prove to this girl that— wonderful things did happen in life, that—fairy godmothers were real, that—rich people had hearts, and that women *were* sisters."
Organization		
Review your body paragraphs. Identify and annotate any sentences that don't flow in a clear and logical way.	Rewrite the sentences so they appear in a logical sequence. Include transitions that clarify the organization of your ideas. Delete details that are repetitive or not essential to support the claim.	Rosemary abandons Miss Smith at the first sign that their friendship could lead to a rivalry for her husband's attention. Later, Rosemary asks her husband to reassure her. "'Philip,' she whispered, and she pressed his head against her bosom, 'am I *pretty*?'" ~~Rosemary abandons Miss Smith at the first sign of that their friendship could lead to a rivalry for her husband's attention.~~ As the story concludes, Miss Smith has been alienated by the woman who claimed to be her benefactor, and Rosemary feels insecure in her relationship with her husband.

Review	Revise	Example
Style: Word Choice		
Identify any sentences that use informal diction. Look for everyday words and phrases that could be replaced with more formal terms.	Replace everyday language with formal, academic language.	By comparing the evening to a patient about to have surgery, Eliot ~~goes against the reader's~~ upends expectations ~~for how natural imagery will work in the poem~~.
Style: Sentence Fluency		
Read your literary analysis essay aloud. Annotate places where the sentences do not flow naturally.	Revise choppy sentences by linking them together. Shorten longer, unfocused sentences to make the key idea clear.	Instead, she views the interaction as a game to keep herself entertained on a rainy day~~., which~~ This becomes clear when she abruptly throws Miss Smith out after her husband, Philip, comments on the young woman's beauty.

✏️ WRITE

Use the revision guide, as well as your peer reviews, to help you evaluate your argumentative literary analysis essay to determine areas that should be revised.

Skill:
Using a Style Guide

••• CHECKLIST FOR USING A STYLE GUIDE

In order to ensure that your work conforms to the guidelines in a style manual, do the following:

- Determine which style guide you should use.

- Use the style guide for the overall formatting of your paper, citation style, bibliography format, and other style considerations for reporting research.

- As you draft, use an additional style guide, such as *Artful Sentences: Syntax as Style* by Virginia Tufte or *The Elements of Style* by William Strunk Jr. and E. B. White, to help you vary your syntax, or the grammatical structure of sentences.

  > Use a variety of simple, compound, complex, and compound-complex sentences to convey information.

  > Be sure to punctuate your sentences correctly.

  > Follow standard English language conventions to help you maintain a formal style for formal papers.

To edit your work so that it conforms to the guidelines in a style manual, consider the following questions:

- Have I followed the conventions for spelling, punctuation, capitalization, sentence structure, and formatting, according to the style guide?

- Have I varied my syntax to make my paper engaging for readers?

- Do I have an entry in my works cited or bibliography for each reference I used?

- Have I followed the correct style, including the guidelines for capitalization and punctuation, in each entry in my works cited or bibliography?

Please note that excerpts and passages in the StudySync® library and this workbook are intended as touchstones to generate interest in an author's work. The excerpts and passages do not substitute for the reading of entire texts, and StudySync® strongly recommends that students seek out and purchase the whole literary or informational work in order to experience it as the author intended. Links to online resellers are available in our digital library. In addition, complete works may be ordered through an authorized reseller by filling out and returning to StudySync® the order form enclosed in this workbook.

Reading & Writing Companion   **139**

YOUR TURN

Read the style questions in the chart below. Then, complete the chart by identifying the header for a section of a style guide that would most likely contain the information needed to answer the question. Write the corresponding letter for each header in the appropriate row.

Style Guide Section Headers	
A	How to Cite Information If No Page Numbers Are Available
B	Words and Expressions Commonly Misused
C	Omit Needless Words
D	How to Cite Plays
E	Form the Singular Possessive of Nouns

Style Question	Section Header
Should I use *affect* or *effect*?	
How do I format dialogue from a drama?	
Should I write "Charles's friend" or "Charles' friend"?	
How do I cite information from a website?	
How do I make my writing more succinct?	

WRITE

Use the checklist to help you choose a convention that has been challenging for you to follow. Use a credible style guide to correct any errors related to that convention in your essay.

Grammar: Commonly Misspelled Words

By following a few simple steps, you can learn how to spell new words—even words that are unfamiliar or difficult. As you write, keep a list of words that you have trouble spelling. Refer to online or print resources for pronunciation, Latin or Greek roots, and other information that may help you remember how the words are spelled. Then, use the steps below to learn the spelling of those words.

Say it. Look at the word again, and say it aloud. Say it again, pronouncing each syllable clearly.

See it. Close your eyes. Picture the word. Visualize it letter by letter.

Write it. Look at the word again, and write it two or three times. Then, write the word without looking at the printed version.

Check it. Check your spelling. Did you spell it correctly? If not, repeat each step until you can spell it easily.

Here are some words that can sometimes confuse even strong spellers

Commonly Misspelled Words		
abundant	accompaniment	against
apparatus	arctic	behavior
business	calendar	cemetery
circumstantial	deference	definite
exhibition	financier	forty
magnificence	metaphor	necessity
playwright	reference	repetitive
seize	sufficient	surprise
transparent	undoubtedly	unnecessary
vaccine	versatile	villain

⟳ YOUR TURN

1. How should this sentence be changed?

> No matter what the calender says today's date is, the weather feels absolutely arctic.

- ○ A. No matter what the calander says today's date is, the weather feels absolutely arctic.
- ○ B. No matter what the calendar says today's date is, the weather feels absolutely arctic.
- ○ C. No matter what the calaendar says today's date is, the weather feels absolutely artic.
- ○ D. No change needs to be made to this sentence.

2. How should this sentence be changed?

> Aunt Polly, who had gotten her degree in poetry, was always quick to seize upon a metaphor.

- ○ A. Aunt Polly, who had gotten her degree in poetry, was always quick to sieze upon a metaphor.
- ○ B. Aunt Polly, who had gotten her degree in poetry, was always quick to seise upon a metafor.
- ○ C. Aunt Polly, who had gotten her degree in poetry, was always quick to seize upon a metaphore.
- ○ D. No change needs to be made to this sentence.

3. How should this sentence be changed?

> Dr. Mason insists that the vacine against influenza is an important part of an annual checkup.

- ○ A. Dr. Mason insists that the vaccene agenst influenza is an important part of an annual checkup.
- ○ B. Dr. Mason insists that the vaccine against influenza is an important part of an annual checkup.
- ○ C. Dr. Mason insists that the vacine aggainst influenza is an important part of an annual checkup.
- ○ D. No change needs to be made to this sentence.

4. How should this sentence be changed?

> Undoubtedley in deferense to my grandfather's wishes, my family planned to hold his birthday dinner at his favorite restaurant.

- ○ A. Undoutedley in defence to my grandfather's wishes, my family planned to hold his birthday dinner at his favorite restaurant.
- ○ B. Undoubtedley in defrence to my grandfather's wishes, my family planned to hold his birthday dinner at his favorite restaurant.
- ○ C. Undoubtedly in deference to my grandfather's wishes, my family planned to hold his birthday dinner at his favorite restaurant.
- ○ D. No change needs to be made to this sentence.

Grammar: Pronoun Case and Reference

Pronouns have four properties: number, person, gender, and case. There are three cases: subject (or nominative), object (or objective), and possessive case. Writers frequently make pronoun-case errors when there are multiple subjects (compound subjects) or multiple objects (compound objects) in a sentence.

Correctly Edited	Incorrect	Explanation
He and Joseph started a charity to help stray cats.	Him and Joseph started a charity to help stray cats.	"Him and Joseph" are the *subjects* of this sentence. "Him" is incorrect because "Him" is in the *object* case.
Read this book and tell Mr. Tannenbaum and **me** what you think.	Read this book and tell Mr. Tannenbaum and I what you think.	"Mr. Tannenbaum and I" are *objects* in this sentence. "I" is incorrect because "I" is in the *subject* case.
I know that **she** and her sister traveled through South America last year.	I know that her and her sister traveled through South America last year.	"Her and her sister" are *subjects* in a clause. The first "her" is incorrect because "her" is in the *object* case. The second "her," however, is correct because it is in the *possessive* case, showing a relationship to the sister.

Sentences that use pronouns can become confusing for a reader if the pronouns do not have clear antecedents. Strong writing avoids ambiguity.

Correctly Edited	Incorrect	Strategy for Revision
The team captain told Karen to take **the captain's** guard position.	The team captain told Karen to take her guard position.	Replace a pronoun with a noun.
Lock the car after you put it in the garage.	When you put the car in the garage, don't forget to lock it.	Rewrite the sentence to make the antecedent clear.

♻ YOUR TURN

1. How should this sentence be changed?

> The committee awarded the band, the female vocalist, and him a music trophy.

- ○ A. They awarded the band, the female vocalist, and him a music trophy.
- ○ B. The committee awarded the band, she, and him a music trophy.
- ○ C. The committee awarded the band, the female vocalist, and he a music trophy.
- ○ D. No change needs to be made to this sentence.

2. How should this sentence be changed?

> The exam that Ms. Standjord is giving to us on Wednesday will be simple for you and I.

- ○ A. The exam that Ms. Standjord is giving to we on Wednesday will be simple for you and I.
- ○ B. The exam that Ms. Standjord is giving to us on Wednesday will be simple for you and me.
- ○ C. The exam that Ms. Standjord is giving to us on Wednesday will be simple for she and I.
- ○ D. No change needs to be made to this sentence.

3. How should this sentence be changed?

> Charlotte emailed Olivia, who was away on a business trip, to say that her mother had been in an automobile accident.

- ○ A. Charlotte emailed she, who was away on a business trip, to say that her mother had been in an automobile accident.
- ○ B. Charlotte emailed Olivia, who was away on a business trip, to say that Olivia's mother had been in an automobile accident.
- ○ C. She emailed Olivia, who was away on a business trip, to say that her mother had been in an automobile accident.
- ○ D. No change needs to be made to this sentence.

Literary Analysis Writing Process: Edit and Publish

PLAN	DRAFT	REVISE	EDIT AND PUBLISH

You have revised your literary analysis based on your peer feedback and your own examination.

Now, it is time to edit your literary analysis. When you revised, you focused on the content of your literary analysis. You probably looked at your essay's claim and thesis statement, your organization, and your supporting evidence. When you edit, you focus on the mechanics of your literary analysis, paying close attention to things like grammar and punctuation.

Use the checklist below to guide you as you edit:

☐ Have I followed relevant rules in the style guide?

☐ Do my pronouns reflect the correct case and have clear antecedents?

☐ Do I have any sentence fragments or run-on sentences?

☐ Have I spelled everything correctly?

Notice some edits Emma has made:

- Fixed a spelling error

- Replaced an unclear pronoun with a noun

- Added a slash to show a line break in a quotation from a poem, and cited line numbers

Please note that excerpts and passages in the StudySync® library and this workbook are intended as touchstones to generate interest in an author's work. The excerpts and passages do not substitute for the reading of entire texts, and StudySync® strongly recommends that students seek out and purchase the whole literary or informational work in order to experience it as the author intended. Links to online resellers are available in our digital library. In addition, complete works may be ordered through an authorized reseller by filling out and returning to StudySync® the order form enclosed in this workbook.

Reading & Writing Companion 145

By comparing the evening to a patient about to have surgery, Eliot upends expectations. This makes readers uncomfortable because they do not know what will happen on the journey on which they are about to ~~embarck~~ embark with ~~him~~ the poem's speaker.

Uncertainty and alienation are also reflected in the speaker himself. He constantly doubts his own worth and place in the world. Instead of simply interacting with people, he stops to ask~~:~~, ~~Do I dare Disturb the universe?~~ "Do I dare / Disturb the universe?" (51-52).

WRITE

Use the questions in the checklist, as well as your peer reviews, to help you evaluate your literary analysis to determine places that need editing. Then, edit your literary analysis to correct those errors.

Once you have made all your corrections, you are ready to publish your work. You can distribute your writing to family and friends, hang it on a bulletin board, or post it on your blog. If you publish online, share the link with your family, friends, and classmates.

Fear of Missing Out

INFORMATIONAL TEXT

Introduction

With countless dating websites and apps, single people have plenty of opportunities to meet their soul mates. But psychologists say that all this choice might not be helpful after all. This article explains the paradox of choice and how it might influence dating in the 21st century.

VOCABULARY

myriad
large number; multitude

paralyze
to make someone or something unable to move

anxiety
a painful or uneasy feeling about something

compatibility
the state of being able to get along without conflict

paradox
a statement that is seemingly contradictory or impossible and yet often reveals a larger truth

NOTES

☰ READ

1   Imagine you are on a date. The person is nice and attractive. You're having a good time. But you wonder if you could be having a better time with someone else. Besides, this person doesn't share your love of 90s hip-hop! Time to use that matchmaking app to find a different date for next weekend.

2   Such is the state of dating in the 21st century. There are more ways than ever to meet people, from dating sites to matchmaking services to location-based apps. That means there are always countless people out there just waiting to meet you. Why settle down when you can swipe right?

3   Making choices is hard. Not only do we struggle to choose from a **myriad** of options, but we also stress after the decision is made over whether or not it was the right one. For example, if you go to a grocery store that has only one type of breakfast cereal available, you buy it. If it's bad, then it's the store's fault for carrying only that one item. But if you buy a bad box from a store chock-full of cereal varieties, whose fault is it? Yours. And that causes **anxiety**.

4   The same goes for online dating. The sheer number of potential online matches can leave daters second-guessing their choices. They wonder if they could have done better. Having two or more equally enticing options causes stress and anxiety. Sometimes people are unable to make any choice at all. If you do choose, you live in constant fear that the other option was better. This condition is known as the **paradox** of choice.

5   Research supports the idea that choice is not always a good thing. In a famous experiment, conducted by Columbia University psychologist Sheena Iyengar, researchers set up a table in a grocery store. In two conditions, people were offered either six or 24 varieties of gourmet jam to taste and purchase. Researchers found that the number of varieties did not change how many people tasted the jam. Surprisingly, however, only three percent of people who were offered 24 varieties purchased a jar. But 30 percent of people offered six varieties purchased a jar. Researchers concluded that more options is not better for decision-making.

6   Likewise, researchers Amitai Shenhav and Randy Buckner put people in an fMRI scanner. They were asked to choose between two objects. The objects were either both high in value (for example, a camera and an MP3 player), both low in value (a bag of pretzels and a water bottle), or of opposite values (a camera and a bag of pretzels). The researchers found that when forced to choose between two high-value objects, people found the decision very hard. Afterward, they felt anxiety over whether they made the right choice.

7   And yet, online dating does lead to successful long-term relationships. According to a study from the University of Chicago, one third of U.S. couples who married between 2005 and 2012 met online. In addition, those couples were less likely to divorce. They were more likely to report being happy in their marriages.

8   Some experts use those statistics and others to show that the paradox of choice is overblown. They say that if having choices were really so **paralyzing** for people, why would we have entire aisles devoted to cereal varieties? In some cases, people seem to like having more options.

9   Some researchers theorize that the reason people go on dates with so many different online matches is not the number of available daters. Rather, it's because of the type of information on online dating profiles. It's not what potential partners really need to know for **compatibility**. A dating profile cannot realistically reflect personality. It cannot show how you interact with others. You must meet someone in person for that. A picture and a location is no substitute for chemistry.

Please note that excerpts and passages in the StudySync® library and this workbook are intended as touchstones to generate interest in an author's work. The excerpts and passages do not substitute for the reading of entire texts, and StudySync® strongly recommends that students seek out and purchase the whole literary or informational work in order to experience it as the author intended. Links to online resellers are available in our digital library. In addition, complete works may be ordered through an authorized reseller by filling out and returning to StudySync® the order form enclosed in this workbook.

Reading & Writing Companion   149

First Read

Read "Fear of Missing Out." After you read, complete the Think Questions below.

☁ THINK QUESTIONS

1. What is the paradox of choice? Explain in your own words. Use textual evidence to support your explanation.

   Paradox of choice is_____

   _____.

2. How has technology changed dating? Cite textual evidence to support your answer.

   Technology has changed dating _____

   _____.

3. Explain the jam study. What did researchers test, and what did they find? Support your answer with textual evidence.

   The jam study was _____.

   Researchers tested _____.

4. Use context to determine the meaning of the word *myriad* as it is used in "Fear of Missing Out." Write your definition of *myriad* here.

   Myriad means _____.

   A context clue is _____.

5. Use context to determine the meaning of the word *anxiety* as it is used in "Fear of Missing Out." Write your definition of *anxiety* here.

   Anxiety means _____.

   A context clue is _____.

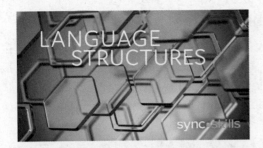

Skill:
Language Structures

★ DEFINE

In every language, there are rules that tell how to **structure** sentences. These rules define the correct order of words. In the English language, for example, a **basic** structure for sentences is subject, verb, and object. Some sentences have more **complicated** structures.

You will encounter both basic and complicated **language structures** in the classroom materials you read. Being familiar with language structures will help you better understand the text.

••• CHECKLIST FOR LANGUAGE STRUCTURES

To improve your comprehension of language structures, do the following:

 Monitor your understanding.

- Ask yourself: Why do I not understand this sentence? Is it because the sentence is long? Or is it because I do not understand the logical relationship between ideas in this sentence?

- Pay attention to coordinating conjunctions.

  > **Coordinating conjunctions** show an equal emphasis on the ideas in a sentence.

  > Some examples of coordinating conjunctions are and, but, and or.

- Pay attention to subordinating conjunctions.

  > **Subordinating conjunctions** show that one idea is more important and the other idea is less important, or subordinate.

  > Some examples of subordinating conjunctions are after, instead, and once.

- Break down the sentence into its parts.

- Ask yourself: How does the writer use conjunctions to combine sentences? Can I break the sentence down into two shorter sentences?

✓ Confirm your understanding with a peer or teacher.

⟳ YOUR TURN

Read each sentence below from "Fear of Missing Out." Then, complete the chart by sorting the sentences into those that use coordinating conjunctions and those that use subordinating conjunctions.

	Sentences
A	They say that if having choices were really so paralyzing for people, why would we have entire aisles devoted to cereal varieties?
B	Not only do we struggle to choose from a myriad of options, but we also stress after the decision is made over whether or not it was the right one.
C	The objects were either both high in value (for example, a camera and an MP3 player), both low in value (a bag of pretzels and a water bottle), or of opposite values (a camera and a bag of pretzels).
D	If it's bad, then it's the store's fault for carrying only that one item.

Coordinating Conjunctions	Subordinating Conjunctions

Skill:
Supporting Evidence

★ DEFINE

In some informational or argumentative texts, the author may share an opinion. This **opinion** may be the author's **claim** or **thesis**. The author must then provide readers with **evidence** that supports their opinion. Supporting evidence can be details, examples, or facts that agree with the author's claim or thesis.

Looking for supporting evidence can help you confirm your understanding of what you read. Finding and analyzing supporting evidence can also help you form your own opinions about the subject.

••• CHECKLIST FOR SUPPORTING EVIDENCE

In order to find and analyze supporting evidence, do the following:

✓ Identify the topic and the author's claim or thesis.

- Ask yourself: What is this mostly about? What is the author's opinion?

✓ Find details, facts, and examples that support the author's claim or thesis.

- Ask yourself: Is this detail important? How does this detail relate to the thesis or claim?

✓ Analyze the supporting evidence.

- Ask yourself: Is this evidence strong? Do I agree with the evidence?

↻ YOUR TURN

Read each line below from "Fear of Missing Out." Then, complete the chart by deciding if the text is a detail, a fact, or an example to support the claim.

	Lines from Text
A	The researchers found that when forced to choose between two high-value objects, people found the decision very hard.
B	The same goes for online dating. The sheer number of potential online matches can leave daters second-guessing their choices.
C	According to a study from the University of Chicago, one third of U.S. couples who married between 2005 and 2012 met online.
D	Imagine you are on a date. The person is nice and attractive. You're having a good time. But you wonder if you could be having a better time with someone else.
E	There are more ways than ever to meet people, from dating sites to matchmaking services to location-based apps.
F	It's not what potential partners really need to know for compatibility. A dating profile cannot realistically reflect personality.

Details	Facts	Examples

Reading & Writing Companion

Close Read

✏ WRITE

ARGUMENTATIVE: Does online dating cause too much anxiety to be successful? Some say yes. Some say no. The article "Fear of Missing Out" explores this topic. Choose a side and write a paragraph explaining your point of view. Use evidence from the text to support your claim. Pay attention to and edit for plurals.

Use the checklist below to guide you as you write.

☐ Does online dating cause too much anxiety to be successful?

☐ What convinced you to support or disagree with the author's claim?

☐ What evidence supports your position?

Use the sentence frames to organize and write your personal response.

Online dating (does / does not) _____ cause _____.

Research shows that people _____.

According to paragraph _____, "_____".

With online dating, _____.

Other research shows _____.

Overall, the paradox of choice _____.

Please note that excerpts and passages in the StudySync® library and this workbook are intended as touchstones to generate interest in an author's work. The excerpts and passages do not substitute for the reading of entire texts, and StudySync® strongly recommends that students seek out and purchase the whole literary or informational work in order to experience it as the author intended. Links to online resellers are available in our digital library. In addition, complete works may be ordered through an authorized reseller by filling out and returning to StudySync® the order form enclosed in this workbook.

Reading & Writing Companion 155

The Ribbons

FICTION

Introduction

In this fictional letter, a woman named Elizabeth tells a story of growing up in Pennsylvania in the 1820s. Her family is poor, but one day Elizabeth's mother gives her some money to spend as she likes. What will she do with this sudden windfall, and what lifelong lesson can be learned?

V VOCABULARY

dismissive

feeling or showing that something or someone is not worth consideration

frivolous

unnecessary, serving no purpose

correspond

to write to someone

diminish

to be made smaller in size or importance

indulge

to give in to someone's whims or wishes

≡ READ

NOTES

My dear Cora:

1   Thank you for your thoughtful and amusing letter. It brightened up an otherwise dreary day. I was especially intrigued by your story about your niece and her **dismissive** response to the new dresses that you so kindly brought her from Paris. I cannot believe she could only speak of how ugly her old dresses were without a compliment for the new ones. As you may recall, my own childhood was filled with love and laughter, but not money. What I wouldn't have given for dresses from Paris!

2   Because we have been **corresponding** for many years, you know that I love to tell stories of my youth in my small town. I am reminded of one such story now. If you **indulge** my memories, it might be of value to your churlish niece.

3   To help my family keep wood on the fire through the freezing Pennsylvania winters, my mother and I took in sewing. My brother would sit and read to us by candlelight as we sewed. On those nights, the sewing rarely felt like work,

the cold seemed distant, and the hours rushed by. One spring, when the flowers started to grow a little earlier than usual, my family no longer needed extra candles and coal. My mother allowed me to keep some of the money in gratitude for my winter of work.

4   I had never before had any money to my own name. I was filled with excitement at the possibilities. I spent days dreaming about what I should buy with my riches. After a week of rolling the coins about in my hand, I took a ride with Father into town. I grasped my coin purse like I thought it would fall right through the wood cart. The day was bright with new beginnings. I was finally going to enter a shop and choose something for myself—not flour for Mother, nor laces for Father's boots, but something **frivolous** and only for me! As I walked across the square, my friend Mary greeted me. I invited her to join me in my shopping. I thought the presence of a friend would only enhance the joy of the day. As we walked down the road together, I saw a beautiful spool of ribbon in a shop window. I instantly knew I should buy it and use it to improve my favorite hat. I pointed the ribbon out to Mary and she said, "How beautiful! Those ribbons are much prettier than the dingy ones you're wearing now. It will be such a lovely improvement."

5   At that, I felt the color rising in my cheeks. I had been so excited for the new ribbons, but Mary's careless comment hurt me deeply. I bought the ribbons, and they were quite beautiful, but I could never quite recapture the joy I felt when I first saw them in the window. Later, in thinking back on the day, I thought of a line from a book that my brother had read to us that winter. The book was *Hope Leslie* by Catharine Maria Sedgwick: "But it is unnecessary to heighten the glory of day by comparing it with the preceding twilight." The glory of my day of wealth was only **diminished** by thinking of my previous poverty, not enhanced.

6   And that, my dear friend, is what you need to remind your niece. When she is given a new dress, she should not focus on the ratty old one that preceded it. We must all focus on the glory of the present day for its own shining sake, and not think of the darkness til we must.

With love,
Elizabeth

First Read

Read "The Ribbons." After you read, complete the Think Questions below.

☁ **THINK QUESTIONS**

1. Why does Elizabeth share the story of the ribbons?

   Elizabeth shares the story about the ribbons because _____.

2. Why did Mary's comment cause Elizabeth to feel embarrassed? Support your inference with textual evidence

   Elizabeth felt embarrassed because _____

   _____.

3. What is Cora's niece supposed to learn from this story? Support your response with textual evidence.

   Cora's niece is supposed to learn that _____

   _____.

4. Use context to determine the meaning of the word *dismissive* as it is used in "The Ribbons." Write your definition of *dismissive* here.

   Dismissive means _____.

   A context clue is _____.

5. Use context to determine the meaning of the word *correspond* as it is used in "The Ribbons." Write your definition of *correspond* here.

   Correspond means _____.

   A context clue is _____.

Skill:
Analyzing Expressions

 DEFINE

When you read, you may find English expressions that you do not know. An **expression** is a group of words that communicates an idea. Three types of expressions are idioms, sayings, and figurative language. They can be difficult to understand because the meanings of the words are different from their **literal**, or usual, meanings.

An **idiom** is an expression that is commonly known among a group of people. For example, "It's raining cats and dogs" means it is raining heavily. **Sayings** are short expressions that contain advice or wisdom. For instance, "Don't count your chickens before they hatch" means do not plan on something good happening before it happens. **Figurative** language is when you describe something by comparing it with something else, either directly (using the words *like* or *as*) or indirectly. For example, "I'm as hungry as a horse" means I'm very hungry. None of the expressions are about actual animals.

••• CHECKLIST FOR ANALYZING EXPRESSIONS

To determine the meaning of an expression, remember the following:

✓ If you find a confusing group of words, it may be an expression. The meaning of words in expressions may not be their literal meaning.

- Ask yourself: Is this confusing because the words are new? Or because the words do not make sense together?

✓ Determining the overall meaning may require that you use one or more of the following:

- context clues

- a dictionary or other resource

- teacher or peer support

✓ Highlight important information before and after the expression to look for clues.

YOUR TURN

Read the situations below. Then, complete the chart by matching the hyperbolic description that matches each situation.

	Hyperbolic Description
A	My brain is frozen!
B	I aged five years in that waiting room.
C	I nearly died laughing!
D	This hurts so bad that the doctor needs to remove my entire foot.

Situation	Hyperboles
You have to wait a long time at the dentist's office.	
You eat ice cream too fast and get a headache.	
You hit your little toe on a table leg.	
Someone tells you a very funny joke.	

Please note that excerpts and passages in the StudySync® library and this workbook are intended as touchstones to generate interest in an author's work. The excerpts and passages do not substitute for the reading of entire texts, and StudySync® strongly recommends that students seek out and purchase the whole literary or informational work in order to experience it as the author intended. Links to online resellers are available in our digital library. In addition, complete works may be ordered through an authorized reseller by filling out and returning to StudySync® the order form enclosed in this workbook.

Reading & Writing Companion **161**

Skill: Visual and Contextual Support

★ DEFINE

Visual support is an image or an object that helps you understand a text. **Contextual support** is a **feature** that helps you understand a text. By using visual and contextual supports, you can develop your vocabulary so you can better understand a variety of texts.

First, preview the text to identify any visual supports. These might include illustrations, graphics, charts, or other objects in a text. Then, identify any contextual supports. Examples of contextual supports are titles, headers, captions, and boldface terms. Write down your **observations**.

Then, write down what those visual and contextual supports tell you about the meaning of the text. Note any new vocabulary that you see in those supports. Ask your peers and your teacher to **confirm** your understanding of the text.

••• CHECKLIST FOR VISUAL AND CONTEXTUAL SUPPORT

To use visual and contextual support to understand texts, do the following:

- ✓ Preview the text. Read the title, headers, and other features. Look at any images and graphics.

- ✓ Write down the visual and contextual supports in the text.

- ✓ Write down what those supports tell you about the text.

- ✓ Note any new vocabulary that you see in those supports.

- ✓ Create an illustration for the reading and write a descriptive caption.

- ✓ Confirm your observations with your peers and teacher.

⟳ YOUR TURN

Read the following example of correspondence. Then, complete the multiple-choice questions below.

Dear Mom and Dad,

Hello from Camp! How are you? I am doing well but I am exhausted after each long day of activities. Today we defeated the counselors in a game of beach volleyball! They have been the defending champions for the last two weeks. It feels great to win! Now I need to learn chess in order to compete in next week's mind games.

The food in the cafeteria is getting better. They actually served pizza yesterday and it tasted delicious! Can we please go out to eat when I get home in two weeks? I love your cooking, mom, but I think we all deserve a night out!

I miss you,
Charlie

---

1. Which is an example of a *salutation*?

   ○ A. Today we defeated the counselors in a game of beach volleyball!

   ○ B. I miss you,

   ○ C. Dear Mom and Dad,

2. Which sentence is part of the *body* of the letter?

   ○ A. Dear Mom and Dad,

   ○ B. Now I need to learn chess in order to compete in next week's mind games.

   ○ C. I miss you, Charlie

3. Which is an example of a *signature*?

   ○ A. It feels great to win!

   ○ B. I miss you, Charlie

   ○ C. Dear Mom and Dad,

4. Which sentence is written in *first person*?

   ○ A. I am so happy that we decided to send Charlie to camp this summer.

   ○ B. They play so many sports at summer camp.

   ○ C. He learned how to play chess!

Please note that excerpts and passages in the StudySync® library and this workbook are intended as touchstones to generate interest in an author's work. The excerpts and passages do not substitute for the reading of entire texts, and StudySync® strongly recommends that students seek out and purchase the whole literary or informational work in order to experience it as the author intended. Links to online resellers are available in our digital library. In addition, complete works may be ordered through an authorized reseller by filling out and returning to StudySync® the order form enclosed in this workbook.

Reading & Writing Companion   163

Close Read

 WRITE

PERSONAL NARRATIVE: The narrator in "The Ribbons" explores the memory of a lesson learned from a bittersweet experience. Write a letter to a friend or family member explaining your experience with this main idea from the text. Include specific details from your life for support. Pay attention to and edit for negatives and contractions.

Use the checklist below to guide you as you write.

☐ What bittersweet experience helped you learn a lesson?

☐ Who was involved in this experience?

☐ What did you learn from this experience?

Use the sentence frames to organize and write your personal narrative.

_____,

How are you? I heard that you _____.

Did you _____? I learned _____ when I _____.

One day _____ said, "_____."

I thought, "_____."

Unfortunately, I _____ and _____.

It was very _____.

I hope you learn from my experience!

_____.

PHOTO/IMAGE CREDITS:

studysync®

Text Fulfillment Through StudySync

If you are interested in specific titles, please fill out the form below and we will check availability through our partners.

ORDER DETAILS

Date:

TITLE	AUTHOR	Paperback/ Hardcover	Specific Edition *If Applicable*	Quantity

SHIPPING INFORMATION

Contact:

Title:

School/District:

Address Line 1:

Address Line 2:

Zip or Postal Code:

Phone:

Mobile:

Email:

BILLING INFORMATION ☐ *SAME AS SHIPPING*

Contact:

Title:

School/District:

Address Line 1:

Address Line 2:

Zip or Postal Code:

Phone:

Mobile:

Email:

PAYMENT INFORMATION

☐ CREDIT CARD

Name on Card:

Card Number:

Expiration Date:

Security Code:

☐ PO

Purchase Order Number:

StudySync Text Fulfillment, BookheadEd Learning, LLC
610 Daniel Young Drive | Sonoma, CA 95476